THE COMPLETE MEDITERRANEAN COOKBOOK 2019 EDITION

1001 Vibrant, Juicy & Delicious Recipes For Living And Eating Well Every Day, Today And Tomorrow

Alexa Riley Webster

Text copyright © **2019 Alexa Riley Webster** All Rights Reserved.

This document is aimed to provide accurate and reliable information in the light of the selected topic and all covered issues. This book is sold with the idea that the publisher is not required to render an officially permitted, accounting, or otherwise, qualified services. If advice is required in any way, professional or legal, seasoned experts of the profession should be consulted. According to the Declaration of Principles, accepted and approved by the Committee of Publishers and Associations and Committee of the American Bar Association. It is no way legal to duplicate, transmit or reproduce, any portion of this document in either printed or electronic form. Any recording of this publication is strictly restricted, and the storage of this document is also prohibited unless written permission is offered by the publisher. All rights reserved.

Every information given herein is claimed to be consistent and truthful, in case of any liability, with regard to inattention or otherwise, by any use or abuse of processes, policies, or directions contained within is solely the responsibility of the recipient reader. Under no conditions will any blame or legal responsibility be held against the publisher for any damages, monetary loss or reparation, due to the information herein.

The information herein is provided entirely for informational purposes, and it is universal. The information is provided without any type of guarantee assurance or a contract.

The trademarks that are used within the document are without any consent, and the publication of the trademark is without the backing of the trademark owner or any support. All brands and trademarks used within this book are to clarify the text only, and they are owned by their owners, not affiliated with this publication.

Respective authors of the publication own all copyrights not held by the publisher.

TABLE OF CONTENT

Introduction 6
Basics of the Mediterranean Diet 7
   What is the Mediterranean Diet? 7
   The scientific basis of the Mediterranean diet 7
   Health benefits of the Mediterranean diet 7
   1. Controlled Blood Cholesterol level 8
   2. Prevents cardiovascular diseases 8
   3. Treatment of Cancer 8
   4. Lowers the Risk of Alzheimer and Parkinson 8
   5. Vitality 8
Eating on the Mediterranean Diet 9
   What to have on a Mediterranean diet? 9
   Food Items from Plant Based sources: 9
   Other Items to use: 9
Setting up the Pantry on a Mediterranean diet: 9
What to Avoid on a Mediterranean Diet? 12
Breakfast Recipes 13
   Green Poached Egg Toasts 14
   Mushroom Egg muffins 15
   Souffle Omelet with Mushrooms 16
   Sweet Potato Breakfast Hash 17
   Spinach Parmesan Baked Eggs 18
   Spinach and Mozzarella Frittata 19
   Crustless Vegetable Quic he 20
   Spinach and Feta Baked Egg 21
   Egg & Spinach Bowls 22
   Tofu Egg Scramble 23
   Egg Stuffed Portobel lo Mushroom 24
   Greek Egg Muffins 25

- Baked Kale and Eggs with Ricotta 26
- Avocado and Egg Breakfast Sandwich 27
- Ham, and Poached Egg English Muffin 28

Smoothie Recipes 29
- Mango smoothie 30
- Beetroot smoothie 31
- Avocado smoothie 32
- Red smoothie 33
- Green smoothie 34
- Kale smoothie 35
- Melon Smoothie 36
- Pineapple smoothie 37
- Kiwi smoothie.. 38
- Mediterranean Smoothie 39
- Coconut Milk Smoothie 40
- Creamy Strawberry Smoothie 41
- Blueberry Banana Smoothie 42
- Basic Breakfast Smoothie 43
- Pina Colada Smoothie... 44

Poultry Recipes 45
- Mediterranean Chicken & Orzo 46
- Chicken & White Bean Soup 47
- Greek Chicken with Roasted Spring Vegetables 48
- Chicken with Tomato Sauce 50
- Souvlaki Kebabs with Vegetable Couscous 52
- Hasselback Caprese Chicken 54
- Turkey Burgers with Feta & Tzatziki 56
- Mediterranean Chicken Quinoa Bowl 58
- Chicken & Spinach Soup with Fresh Pesto 60
- Mediterranean Chicken with Potatoes 62
- Olive Chicken 64

Cheesy Chicken with Tomatoes	66
Roasted Mediterranean Chicken	68
Chicken & Winter Squash	70
Lemon-Thyme Chicken	72

Beef, Pork and Lamb Recipes ... 74

Pork Tenderloin with Orzo	75
Pork Chops	76
Garlic and Rosemary Mediterranean Pork Roast	78
Mediterranean Pork Medallions	79
Blue Cheese-Topped Pork Chops	80
Roasted Pepper Meat Loaf	81
Herbed Beef Skewers	82
Vegetables Lamb Shanks	83
Grilled London Broil	85
Lamb Pasta & Cheese	86
Spinach Beef Pinwheels	88
Romesco Glazed Beef Steak	90
Mint Beef Skewers	92
Baked Lamb Tray	93

Soup Recipes ... 94

Cannellini Beans Soup	95
Red Barley Soup	97
Tuscan Bean Soup	99
Ditalini Minestrone	101
Greek Meatball Soup	103
Zucchini Soup	105
Grilled Vegetable soup	107
Napoletana Hoki soup	108
White Celeriac soup	109
Passata Cream Soup	110
Tortellini soup	111

Potato Mushroom Soup 112

Fish and Seafood Recipes 113

Mixed Seafood Stew 114

Squid Oyster Medley 116

Sauce Dipped Mussels 118

Crusty Grilled mussels 119

Seafood Garlic Couscous 120

Lobster Rice Paella 121

Fish and Vegetable Parcels 123

Seafood with Couscous Salad 124

Saffron Fish gratins 125

Beans Recipes 127

Spinach Beans 128

Meatballs Chickpea Medley 129

Black Beans Feta Salad 130

Chickpeas Pepper Salad 131

Juicy Red Bean Salad 132

Basil Butter Beans 133

Citrus Garlic Beans 134

Greek StockBeans 135

Meatball Beans Stew 136

Bean Mash with Grilled Veggies 137

Side and Snacks 138

Mediterranean sardine salad 139

Niçoise toasts 140

Herbed Olives 142

Stuffed tomatoes 143

Aubergine & pepper salad 144

Crispy squid with capers 145

Spiced tortilla 146

Garlic bread pizzas 147

- Easy tomato pizzas 148
- Goat's cheese pizza 149

Vegetarian Recipes 150
- Griddled vegetable & feta tart 151
- Mediterranean gnocchi 152
- Lemony mushroom & herb rice 153
- Cashew Rice 154
- Parmesan Roasted Broccoli 155
- Baked Goat Cheese with Tomato Sauce 156
- Roasted Vegetable Tabbouleh 157
- Vegan Pesto Spaghetti Squash 158
- Charred Green Beans with Mustard 159
- Smoky Roasted Vegetables 160

Dessert Recipes 161
- Banana Greek Yogurt Bowl 162
- Popped Quinoa Bars 163
- Greek Baklava 164
- Orange Sesame Cookies 165
- Honey yogurt cheesecake 166
- Fruity Almond cake 167
- Almond Orange Pandoro 168
- Blueberry & macadamia flapjacks 169
- Compote Dipped Berries Mix 170
- Honey Glazed Pears 171

Conversion Tables 172
- Butter or Superfine Sugar 172
- Granulated Sugar, Light or Dark Brown Sugar 172
- All-purpose or Bread Flour 172
- Cake & Pastry Flour, Icing Sugar, Rice Flour or Breadcrumbs 172
- Cocoa Powder, Corn Starch, Ground Almonds 172
- Rolled Oats, Whole Pecans, Whole Walnuts 173
- Other Ingredients 173
- Small Measure Items 173

Conclusion 174

INTRODUCTION

A diet that can ensure good health is surely the need of everyone these days. Especially the with organic content and simply easy recipes. Such is the Mediterranean diet, it can offer a mix of all the nutrients in a single menu, and a balance is what we seek today when it comes to our food and routine. With all the ingredients in proportion, we can keep our metabolism in check. People stuck in several ifs and buts when it comes to following a specific diet plan, so it is imperative to have complete clarity of the diet we follow. The Mediterranean due to its sheer simplicity makes this process easier for everyone; it restricts food consumption in a way that it does not feel giving so much out of your routine meal. it simply alters our eating habits but introducing more vegetables, fruits, and grain into our diet and cutting out more of the processed food, table sugars, and refined food items. It recommends more organic food and less manufactured products. Through the text of this book, we will look deeper into the basics of the Mediterranean diet, the origin of the diet, its benefits, its recommendations and lastly several of the quick and easy to cook Mediterranean recipes. Together all the sections of this book will provide a yardstick to measure Mediterranean diet standards.

WHAT IS THE MEDITERRANEAN DIET?

The word the Mediterranean itself is quite reflecting of the diet's origin. The region surrounding the Mediterranean Sea has a culinary culture of its own and from the diet came to a rise. Countries including France, Span, Italy, and Greece, are all encircling the Mediterranean Sea and they all share similarities in their culinary traditions. the consumption of legumes, nuts, vegetables, beans, fish, poultry, cereal, whole grains, and plant-based fats has always been common in this region. the good health of the people living in those places later became an inspiration for the world, and everyone believed in the importance of the Mediterranean diet. Since then the diet has been used by most people around the world to take more vitamins, fibers, and balanced nutrients in their meal and to maintain good health. this diet is also free from bad cholesterol, so it is also significant in preventing and curing several of the health conditions.

THE SCIENTIFIC BASIS OF THE MEDITERRANEAN DIET

The concept of the Mediterranean diet lies in a simple term "Plant Based," everything plant-based holds more value in this diet, whether it is fats, fruits, nuts or vegetables. To make it more comprehensive and enriched, the plant-based ingredients are paired with some of the animal-based products like the seafood, meat, and dairy. Balance is the key to all this, with the mind of limiting every nutrient to create an equal proportion you can achieve the objectives of the Mediterranean diet. This is the reason that researchers from all over the world have termed it as the 'The best ever" as it is health oriented but simple enough for anyone to opt in their routine.

It was early scientific studies on the Mediterranean diet and the people taking it which lead to its better recognition. They found out that people on this diet can better resist to effects of aging, gut problems, mental ailments, cardiovascular diseases, skin issues, and genetic disorders. Since the diet is less on bad cholesterol, a group of researchers found its low-fat content reasonably beneficial for all the people suffering from high blood cholesterol, high blood pressure, and several heart diseases. this diet has also been seen as most effective it extending the average expectancy of the people living in the Mediterranean region. for these many reasons, the Mediterranean diet is looked at by many in the world as a way forward for great health.

HEALTH BENEFITS OF THE MEDITERRANEAN DIET

It is not natural to instantly opt for a diet without knowing its actual impacts on your mind and body. This why we shall discover all the healthy benefits of the Mediterranean to establish its significance. Since the Mediterranean is not termed as a cuisine, but it is claimed as a diet, which means it draws out a map to attain certain health objectives through alteration in eating habits and type of the food we eat, that is why is only just to say that the Mediterranean diet can help you achieve following health-related targets:

1. CONTROLLED BLOOD CHOLESTEROL LEVEL

It is the low-density lipoproteins or the LDL which cause obstruction of the blood vessels by creating a clog. These are therefore termed as the bad cholesterols. All such cholesterols are present in processed animal fats or saturated fats, the Mediterranean cuts the use of any of such items which could contain LDL, and hence it proved to be miraculous in preventing diseases like high blood pressure or cholesterol or cardiac disorders.

2. PREVENTS CARDIOVASCULAR DISEASES

The Mediterranean diet works in different ways to prevent cardiovascular diseases and also helps to contain the diseases. firstly it restricts the use of fats and its type, which results in an unhindered flow of the blood in the body, meaning no extra pressure on the cardiac muscles. Secondly, it also strengthens the vascular system by providing it essential proteins and necessary vitamins and minerals which prevents the weakening of the heart walls and valves. It also regulates the release of the hormones in the body and the functioning of the enzymes in a balanced manner.

3. TREATMENT OF CANCER

Cancer is one word which creates a shiver down your spine when you think of catching the disease. The so-called incurable diseases can be prevented and sometimes even treated with the right diet. And there is no better diet than the Mediterranean to prevent such a disease. The fruits and vegetable-rich meals can provide all the detoxifiers which prevent any mutation in the body cells which is normally the cause of cancer. This supports and strengthens the body's own mechanism so well, that its waves off any external influence to alter its chemistry.

4. LOWERS THE RISK OF ALZHEIMER AND PARKINSON

Many people have fought against Parkinson and Alzheimer through Mediterranean diet. this diet has been proved effective in normalizing the brain activities. The nutrients, vitamins, and minerals provided through this diet help to nourish and brain cells which can possibly revive its normal functioning. Its detoxification quality also creates an impact to remove all the brain-damaging agents out of the body. Metabolic waste is released out of the body.

5. VITALITY

Vitality is the proven effect of the Mediterranean diet. with a proportionate amount of the nutrients and energy provided to the body cells, their life is prolonged. They can actively metabolize and live longer than visual. Moreover, the diet is also linked to all the body's mechanism from cardiovascular to gut and the brain, its positive impact over all of these is another factor which promotes long and healthy life.

WHAT TO HAVE ON A MEDITERRANEAN DIET?

While in this so-called industrialized age, it is hard to imagine living without manufactured or mass-produced food items, but this is what the Mediterranean diet is all about. it prescribes health through the use of natural and organic food, which contains mostly plant-based ingredients whether it's the legumes, grains, nuts, seeds, fruits, and vegetables. Down below is a comprehensive list of the ingredients which are exclusively used in a pure Mediterranean diet.

1. Food Items from Plant Based sources:
   - Whole grains
   - Vegetables
   - Fruits
   - Legumes
   - Nuts
   - Canola oil
   - Olive oil
   - Sesame oil
   - Grapeseed oil

(Note: All the saturated fats have to be avoided which includes butter and ghee etc.)

Other Items to use:
1. Dried or fresh herbs
2. All the spices, whole or ground.
3. Whole wheat flour, almond or coconut flour.
4. Lean meat can be used but only two times a week.
5. Good amount of seafood and fish.

SETTING UP THE PANTRY ON A MEDITERRANEAN DIET

To start with the Mediterranean diet, it is important to first make your mind, set the schedule, buy the diet-oriented groceries and then set your pantry and kitchen shelves with only related food items. By removing the unwanted ingredients from your kitchen, you will be able to stick to your diet easily and with more consistency. That is why it is prescribed to follow the following list of basic items to stuff your kitchen and refrigerator with for the Mediterranean diet. This list contains just basic fruits and vegetables to give an idea. However, any fruit and vegetable can be used on this diet without any restriction.

EATING ON THE MEDITERRANEAN DIET

Vegetables	Fruits	Herbs and Spices	Meat	Grains
Artichokes	Apples	Basil	Chicken	Barley
Beets	Apricot	Bay leaves	Turkey	Bulgur
Bell peppers	Banana	Chiles	No fat beef	Couscous
Broccoli	Berries	Cilantro	Clams	Oatmeal
Cabbage	Figs	Coriander	Cod	Pasta
Eggplant	Oranges	Cumin	Crab	Polenta
Green beans	Dates	Mint	Salmon	Quinoa
Leafy greens	Plums	Parsley	Scallops	Rice
Leeks	Lemons	Rosemary	Shrimp	
Olives	Grapes	Sage	Tuna	
Squash	Melon	Tarragon	Tilapia	
Peas	Peaches	Oregano		
Tomatoes		Pepper		
Garlic		Thyme		
Carrots				
Onions				
mushrooms				

Dairy	Nuts and Seeds	Oils	Beans
Cheese	Almonds	Olive oil	Black beans
Low-fat milk	Cashews	Avocado oil	Chickpeas
Plain or Greek yogurt	Flax	Canola oil	Hummus
eggs	Peanuts	Grape seed oil	Pinto beans
	Pumpkin seeds		Lentils
	Sunflower seeds		White beans
	Walnuts		

WHAT TO AVOID ON A MEDITERRANEAN DIET?

Whether you are dining out or cooking at home, there are certain ingredients you cannot risk taking on the Mediterranean diet. Well, the diet basically emphasizes on what to eat, rather on 'what not to eat' but there are certain restrictions which are important to consider, like avoiding trans fats or solid saturated fats, do not use alcoholic items, and avoid taking high-fat dairy products. Similarly, refined and processed flours are also not openly allowed on a Mediterranean diet. Instead of table sugars, the organic sweeteners like honey, etc. has to be used to keep the ingredients natural and low on carbs. You can easily follow these guidelines when you are cooking at home since you get you set up your own pantry, but it is difficult to keep up with it when you are ordering food in a restaurant. You can never ask for a perfect Mediterranean meal. However, there are certain ways that can save you from crossing into the unsafe zone, and those are:

1. Anything fried can comprise health since you can't be sure of the quality of the fat used. So do not order any item which is fried. Instead, opt for things which are steamed or baked or boiled.
2. It is always safe to order seafood or poultry than ordering red meat since not all places use lean beef, lamb or pork meat.
3. If you are choosing the beef or pork meals to order, ask for thin cut portions like lean sirloin, flanks or steaks. These pieces are free from all the excess fat which can be harmful tohealth.
4. Plant-based oil is suitable for the Mediterranean diet, so any dip or sauce is containing butter or ghee should also be crossed off your list. Avoid ordering all such items.
5. When you are not sure of the meat quality and the type of the ingredients used in other meal, look for dishes with most vegetables those are probably the safest option for everyone.
6. Fresh salads and vegetables mashes are always good to serve as a side meal. They contain all safe and healthy ingredients.
7. Most outdoor desserts contain white sugars or confectionary sugars, so look for something with fruits only like berries, pears or apples, etc.
8. Try ordering the desserts in a small amount to keep your caloric intake in check.
9. Alcohol is not allowed on the Mediterranean diet, so avoid adding any such beverage to your menu.

BREAKFAST RECIPES

Green Poached Egg Toasts
Mushroom Egg muffins
Souffle Omelet with Mushrooms
Sweet Potato Breakfast Hash
Spinach Parmesan Baked Eggs
Spinach and Mozzarella Frittata
Crustless Vegetable Quiche
Spinach and Feta Baked Egg
Egg & Spinach Bowls
Tofu Egg Scramble

THE COMPLETE MEDITERRANEAN COOKBOOK 2019 EDITION

BREAKFAST RECIPES

GREEN POACHED EGG TOASTS

Here is a healthy approach to enjoy the same old morning egg with crispy toasts in a much tempting style. With the freshly mashed avocado flesh and smoked salmon, these toasts bites can give you a kicking start in the morning

Preparation time: 10 minutes	**Cooking time:** 5 minutes	**Allergens:** Egg, soy

INGREDIENTS

- 2 bread slices, toasted
- 2 oz avocado flesh, mashed
- 1/4 tsp lemon juice
- Kosher salt and black pepper, to taste
- 3.5 oz smoked salmon
- 2 eggs
- 1 teaspoon soy sauce

INSTRUCTIONS

1. First, start by boiling the water in the medium-sized pot.
2. Once it is boiled, create a whirlpool in the water and crack the one egg into it until it is cooked.
3. Repeat the same process with another egg and transfer them immediately to an ice bath for 10 seconds.
4. Scoop out the fresh avocado flesh into a bowl and mash it using a fork or spoon. Keep it aside.
5. Place the two toasted slices in the serving plates, spread the avocado mash over them generously.
6. Divide the smoked salmon over the bread slices.
7. Drizzle half of the lemon juice, soy sauce, salt, and pepper over each of the toasts then top each with one poached egg.
8. Enjoy!

NUTRITION FACTS

Servings: 2		
Amount per serving Calories		195
		% Daily Value*
Total Fat	**11.2g**	14%
Saturated Fat	**2.5g**	12%
Cholesterol	**175mg**	58%
Sodium	**1267mg**	55%
Total Carbohydrate	**7.8g**	3%
Dietary Fiber	**2.3g**	8%
Total Sugars	**1g**	
Protein	**16.1g**	
Vitamin D	**15mcg**	77%
Calcium	**49mg**	4%
Iron	**2mg**	10%
Potassium	**313mg**	7%

MUSHROOM EGG MUFFINS

Abandon the traditional egg muffins and enjoy them with the tasty twist of mushrooms and roasted peppers. The strong smoky flavor of these muffins is finger-licking delicious.

Preparation Time: 10 Minutes	**Cooking Time:** 25 Minutes	**Allergens:** Eggs

INGREDIENTS

- cooking spray
- 5 eggs
- 1/3 cup coconut milk
- 1/4 teaspoon garlic powder
- Salt and black pepper to taste
- 1 1/2 cups mushrooms, chopped
- 1 1/2 cups roasted bell peppers, chopped, rinsed and drained

Topping
- Fresh green herbs and red pepper slices

INSTRUCTIONS

1. Preheat the oven to 350° F (177° C).
2. Meanwhile, prepare a 12-cup muffin tray by lining it with cooking spray. Keep it aside.
3. Crack all the eggs in a bowl and whisk them with coconut milk, salt, garlic powder, and black pepper.
4. Once it is mixed, fold in mushrooms and peppers and mix it evenly.
5. Divide the batter into the greased muffin cups equally.
6. Bake the mushroom batter for 20 to 25 minutes until they are firm and set.
7. Once done, allow the muffin tray to cool and then remove the muffins.
8. Garnish them with fresh herbs and red pepper slice.

NUTRITION FACTS

Servings: 4		
Amount per serving		
Calories		216
		% Daily Value*
Total Fat	**15.3g**	20%
Saturated Fat	**9.4g**	47%
Cholesterol	**215mg**	72%
Sodium	**292mg**	13%
Total Carbohydrate	**3.6g**	1%
Dietary Fiber	**0.7g**	3%
Total Sugars	**2.6g**	
Protein	**11.2g**	
Vitamin D	**114mcg**	569%
Calcium	**53mg**	4%
Iron	**2mg**	12%
Potassium	**213mg**	5%

SOUFFLE OMELET WITH MUSHROOMS

This souffle omelet is nothing like your routine morning eggs. It has this soft and spongy texture which is made out of a foamy mixture of egg whites and yolk. Moreover, the mushrooms infilling of this omelet can lit your morning.

Preparation Time: 10 Minutes	**Cooking Time:** 15 Minutes	**Allergens:** Eggs, Dairy

INGREDIENTS

- 1 teaspoon extra-virgin olive oil
- 1 clove garlic, minced
- 8 ounces sliced mushrooms
- 1 tablespoon parsley, minced
- 3 large eggs, separated
- 1/2 teaspoon salt
- 1/2 teaspoon pepper
- 1/4 cup grated cheese

INSTRUCTIONS

1. Warm a nonstick skillet with oil over medium-high heat.
2. Add garlic to sauté for few seconds then stir in mushroom.
3. Stir cook for 10 minutes. Drizzle parsley on top then turn off the heat.
4. Beat egg yolks in a bowl until it thickens.
5. Whisk the egg whites separately until it turns foamy and white.
6. Mix the egg whites with yolks by folding it in.
7. Season this mixture with salt, pepper, and cheese.
8. Warm a large skillet on medium heat.
9. Pour the egg batter in the skillet and cover the lid to cook.
10. Once the bottom is set, spread mushroom over one side of the egg.
11. Fold it over the mushrooms and transfer it to plate.
12. Serve.

NUTRITION FACTS

Servings: 3		
Amount per serving		
Calories		142
		% Daily Value*
Total Fat	9.9g	13%
Saturated Fat	3.8g	19%
Cholesterol	196mg	65%
Sodium	521mg	23%
Total Carbohydrate	3.6g	1%
Dietary Fiber	0.9g	3%
Total Sugars	1.8g	
Protein	11.2g	
Vitamin D	291mcg	1454%
Calcium	100mg	8%
Iron	3mg	19%
Potassium	332mg	7%

SWEET POTATO BREAKFAST HASH

Sweet potatoes are delicious enough to try them any style, and when cooked with some extra seasoning and a mixture of ham and avocado these will melt your heart away.

| **Preparation Time:** 10 Minutes | **Cooking Time:** 20 Minutes | **Allergens:** Eggs |

INGREDIENTS

- 2 sweet potatoes, peeled and cubed
- 3 tablespoons olive oil
- 1/2 teaspoon salt
- 1/4 teaspoon ground white pepper
- 1 tablespoon apple cider vinegar
- 2 cloves garlic, minced
- 1 teaspoon honey
- 1/4 cup yellow onion, diced
- 1/4 cup green bell pepper, diced
- 8 ounces low sodium sulfate free ham, diced
- 1 tablespoon lemon juice
- 1 avocado, peeled, pit removed, and diced

INSTRUCTIONS

1. Layer a baking sheet with tin foil and set the oven to 450° F (232° C).
2. Toss the sweet potatoes with half tablespoon olive oil, pepper, and salt.
3. Spread these seasoned potatoes in the baking sheet and bake them for 15 minutes
4. Combine apple cider vinegar, honey, and garlic in small bowl.
5. While whisking stir in 1 tablespoon olive oil.
6. Warm the skillet over medium heat with remaining olive oil in it.
7. Stir in pepper and onion and sauté until they are soft.
8. Now add baked potatoes and ham. Cook until the ham turns golden.
9. Turn off the heat then season this mixture with vinegar sauce, lemon juice, and avocado.
10. Serve warm.

NUTRITION FACTS

Servings: **3**	
Amount per serving	
Calories	382
	% Daily Value*
Total Fat 23.4g	30%
Saturated Fat 5.7g	29%
Cholesterol 65mg	22%
Sodium 1679mg	73%
Total Carbohydrate 23.4g	9%
Dietary Fiber 6g	21%
Total Sugars 1.9g	
Protein 20.4g	
Vitamin D 0mcg	0%
Calcium 44mg	3%
Iron 2mg	10%
Potassium 923mg	

SPINACH PARMESAN BAKED EGGS

Let's break the routine and try a unique combination of baked eggs with spinach and parmesan. The eggs are baked in the mixture of sautéed spinach, topped with cheese and tomatoes, all hues in a single serving.

Preparation Time: 10 Minutes   **Cooking Time:** 15 Minutes   **Allergens:** Eggs, Dairy

INGREDIENTS

- 2 teaspoons olive oil
- 2 cloves garlic, minced
- 4 cups baby spinach
- 1/2 cup fat-free grated parmesan cheese
- 4 eggs
- 1 small tomato, diced small

NUTRITION FACTS

Servings: 4		
Amount per serving		
Calories		231
		% Daily Value*
Total Fat	15.9g	20%
Saturated Fat	7.7g	39%
Cholesterol	194mg	65%
Sodium	477mg	21%
Total Carbohydrate	4.3g	2%
Dietary Fiber	1g	3%
Total Sugars	1.1g	
Protein	20.2g	
Vitamin D	15mcg	77%
Calcium	433mg	33%
Iron	2mg	10%
Potassium	286mg	6%

INSTRUCTIONS

1. Set the oven on 350° F (177°C) to preheat.
2. Layer an 8-inch casserole dish with cooking spray.
3. Warm olive oil in a large skillet over medium heat.
4. Stir in garlic and spinach, sauté until spinach is wilted.
5. Remove it from the heat then drain off the extra liquid.
6. Add parmesan cheese and transfer this mixture to the casserole dish.
7. Make four wells in the spinach mixture to add eggs.
8. Crack one egg into each well.
9. Place the cooking dish in the oven and bake them for 15 minutes.
10. Serve warm.

BREAKFAST RECIPES

SPINACH AND MOZZARELLA FRITTATA

Slow cooked cheesy frittata is the creamiest treat for your morning breakfast. It is a perfect mix of chopped onions, spinach, tomato, and basic seasoning. Best to serve with toasted warm bread.

| **Preparation Time:** 10 Minutes | **Cooking Time:** 1 hr. 30 minutes | **Allergens:** Eggs, Dairy |

INGREDIENTS

- 1 cup cooked spinach, squeezed to remove water
- 4 eggs
- 1/2 cup fat-free feta cheese

NUTRITION FACTS

Servings: 4		
Amount per serving		
Calories		131
		% Daily Value*
Total Fat	8.3g	11%
Saturated Fat	2.3g	12%
Cholesterol	127mg	42%
Sodium	166mg	7%
Total Carbohydrate	5g	2%
Dietary Fiber	1g	4%
Total Sugars	2.7g	
Protein	10g	
Vitamin D	16mcg	78%
Calcium	45mg	3%
Iron	2mg	11%
Potassium	263mg	6%

INSTRUCTIONS

1. Preheat a small skillet with oil over medium heat.
2. Add onion and sauté for 5 minutes.
3. Grease a slow cooker and prepare it for cooking.
4. Mix sautéed onions with cheese and all the ingredients.
5. Add these ingredients to the slow cooker.
6. Cover the cooker to cook on LOW settings for 1- 1.5 hours.
7. Serve warm.

CRUSTLESS VEGETABLE QUICHE

The crustless vegetable quiche will become the ultimate love for veggies lovers. It is cooked using juicy zucchini, nutritional broccoli, and bell pepper mixture. Beside basic spices, it has the distinct flavors of the dried herbs.

| **Preparation Time:** 10 Minutes | **Cooking Time:** 30 minutes | **Allergens:** Eggs, Dairy |

INGREDIENTS

- 1 tablespoon olive oil
- 1 small yellow onion, diced
- 2 cloves garlic, minced
- ½ cup diced red bell pepper
- ½ cup diced green bell pepper
- ½ cup sliced zucchini
- 6 broccoli florets
- ¼ cup diced sun-dried tomatoes
- 3 large eggs
- 4 large egg whites
- 2 tablespoons coconut milk
- 1 teaspoon dried oregano
- ½ teaspoon black pepper
- Sea Salt to taste
- ¼ cup 1 tablespoon low-fat parmesan cheese, optional

NUTRITION FACTS

Servings: 4	
Amount per serving	
Calories	180
	% Daily Value*
Total Fat 9.9g	13%
Saturated Fat 3.2g	16%
Cholesterol 147mg	49%
Sodium 222mg	10%
Total Carbohydrate 10.4g	4%
Dietary Fiber 2.9g	10%
Total Sugars 4.2g	
Protein 14.5g	
Vitamin D 17mcg	86%
Calcium 176mg	14%
Iron 2mg	10%
Potassium 467mg	10%

INSTRUCTIONS

1. Set the oven at 425° F (218° C) to preheat.
2. Meanwhile, warm a large skillet over medium heat.
3. Add oil and sauté onion and garlic in it for 4 minutes.
4. Stir in zucchini, bell pepper, broccoli and dried tomatoes.
5. Sauté for 2 minutes then add these vegetables to a bowl.
6. Now whisk eggs with milk, spices, egg whites, and ¼ cup parmesan cheese.
7. Stir in sautéed egg mixture and then transfer the batter a 9inch greased pie dish.
8. Loosely cover the pie dish with foil and bake it for 10 minutes at 425° F (218° C).
9. Reduce the heat to 350° F (177° C) then bake for 20 minutes.
10. Drizzle parmesan on top.
11. Serve.

SPINACH AND FETA BAKED EGG

These spinach lined eggs muffin cups are the easiest one to enjoy in no time. No spices and extra ingredients. It is all cheese, eggs, and spinach. Simple to cook yet richer and healthier in content.

Preparation Time: 10 Minutes   **Cooking Time:** 15 minutes   **Allergens:** Eggs, Dairy

INGREDIENTS

- 1 cup cooked spinach, squeezed to remove water
- 4 eggs
- 1/2 cup fat-free feta cheese

INSTRUCTIONS

1. Layer a muffin pan with muffin cups and cooking spray then set it aside.
2. Set the oven at 375° F (190° C) to preheat.
3. First, divide the spinach into four muffin cups. Press it into the bottom.
4. Add whisked eggs and top it with feta.
5. Bake the spinach eggs for 15 minutes.
6. Serve warm.

NUTRITION FACTS

Servings: 4		
Amount per serving		
Calories		114
		% Daily Value*
Total Fat	8.4g	11%
Saturated Fat	4.2g	21%
Cholesterol	180mg	60%
Sodium	277mg	12%
Total Carbohydrate	1.4g	1%
Dietary Fiber	0.2g	1%
Total Sugars	1.1g	
Protein	8.4g	
Vitamin D	15mcg	1%
Calcium	123mg	9%
Iron	1mg	6%
Potassium	112mg	2%

EGG & SPINACH BOWLS

Let's take the traditional egg muffins to a whole new level and prepare a seasoned spinach mixed egg batter in small ramekins to serve at your breakfast table. Always serve after baking for best and experience.

| **Preparation Time:** 10 Minutes | **Cooking Time:** 20 Minutes | **Allergens:** Eggs, Dairy |

INGREDIENTS

- 8 large egg whites, (recommend free-range)
- 1 whole egg
- 1 cup baby spinach, torn or chopped into small pieces
- 1/2 cup diced tomatoes
- 1/4 cup feta cheese, fat-free
- 1/2 teaspoon black pepper
- Kosher or sea salt to taste

INSTRUCTIONS

1. Set the oven at 350° F (177° C).
2. Whisk everything in a suitable bowl until well combined.
3. Spray ramekins with cooking spray.
4. Divide the egg mixture into the ramekins.
5. Bake them for 20 minutes.
6. Serve warm.

NUTRITION FACTS

Servings: 3		
Amount per serving		
Calories		119
		% Daily Value*
Total Fat	4.3g	6%
Saturated Fat	2.3g	12%
Cholesterol	66mg	22%
Sodium	382mg	17%
Total Carbohydrate	6g	2%
Dietary Fiber	2.1g	8%
Total Sugars	2g	
Protein	14.2g	
Vitamin D	5mcg	26%
Calcium	100mg	8%
Iron	2mg	10%
Potassium	246mg	5%

BREAKFAST RECIPES

TOFU EGG SCRAMBLE

Let's make the plain old egg scramble a bit chunkier with the twist of diced tofu, onion, and kale. Vegetables are mixed together and then mixed with whisked egg whites. The scramble can be served with parsley toppings.

| **Preparation Time:** 10 Minutes | **Cooking Time:** 5 Minutes | **Allergens:** Eggs |

INGREDIENTS

- 4 ounces extra firm tofu, cubed
- 1/4 cup red bell pepper, chopped
- 1 tablespoon olive oil
- 1/4 cup red onion, chopped
- 1 cup kale, roughly chopped
- 1/2 teaspoon ground cumin
- 1 teaspoon chili powder
- 6 egg whites, lightly beaten
- 2 tablespoons fresh cilantro, chopped

INSTRUCTIONS

1. Warm the skillet with cooking oil on medium heat.
2. Add tofu, onion, pepper, and kale to the pan.
3. Sauté until the veggies are soft. Season them with cumin and chili powder.
4. Gradually stir in egg whites and cook to make the scramble.
5. Garnish with cilantro.
6. Serve warm.

NUTRITION FACTS

Servings: 3		
Amount per serving		
Calories		123
		% Daily Value*
Total Fat	6.6g	8%
Saturated Fat	1g	5%
Cholesterol	0mg	0%
Sodium	91mg	4%
Total Carbohydrate	5.7g	2%
Dietary Fiber	1.4g	5%
Total Sugars	1.7g	
Protein	11.4g	
Vitamin D	0mcg	0%
Calcium	120mg	9%
Iron	1mg	8%
Potassium	332mg	7%

EGG STUFFED PORTOBELLO MUSHROOM

For a rich and healthy breakfast, these eggs stuffed mushroom caps are a perfect option. These contain all the ingredients of taste and appealing aroma. Moreover, if you have the stuffing preserve in the refrigerator, it hardly takes few minutes to ready it to devour.

| **Preparation Time:** 10 Minutes | **Cooking Time:** 20 Minutes | **Allergens:** Eggs, Dairy |

INGREDIENTS

- 4 large portobello mushrooms, stem removed, wiped clean
- 2 tablespoons olive oil
- 1/2 teaspoon Kosher salt
- 1/4 teaspoon ground black pepper
- 1/4 teaspoon garlic powder
- 4 large eggs
- 2 tablespoons crumbled feta cheese
- 1/4 cup fresh parsley, chopped
- ¼ cup red bell pepper, chopped

INSTRUCTIONS

1. Layer a baking sheet with tin foil and keep it aside.
2. Heat the oven on broiler settings.
3. Rub the mushroom caps with olive oil on both sides.
4. Drizzle half of the salt, pepper and garlic powder.
5. Place the caps in the baking tray and broil them for 5 minutes.
6. Drain the excess liquid from the mushroom.
7. Set the temperature of oven to 400° F (204° C).
8. Crack one egg in each mushroom cap and top it with feta cheese.
9. Bake them for 15 minutes the drizzle salt, garlic powder, and pepper on top.
10. Garnish with parsley and chopped bell pepper.
11. Serve warm.

NUTRITION FACTS

Servings: 4		
Amount per serving		
Calories		205
		% Daily Value*
Total Fat	15.3g	20%
Saturated Fat	4.6g	23%
Cholesterol	196mg	65%
Sodium	504mg	22%
Total Carbohydrate	6.4g	2%
Dietary Fiber	1.8g	7%
Total Sugars	2.1g	
Protein	13.4g	
Vitamin D	18mcg	88%
Calcium	180mg	14%
Iron	2mg	13%
Potassium	570mg	12%

GREEK EGG MUFFINS

The Greek egg muffins are famous for the refreshing combination of the vegetables used in them. It takes tomatoes, onions, and the olives to prepare a nice egg batter for these muffins.

Preparation Time: 10 Minutes **Cooking Time:** 20 Minutes **Allergens:** Eggs, Dairy

INGREDIENTS

- 4 egg whites
- 2 eggs
- 1/2 cup coconut milk
- 1/2 teaspoon salt
- 1/4 teaspoon ground white pepper
- 1/4 cup tomatoes, diced small
- 1/4 cup red onion, diced small
- 1/4 cup black olives, diced small
- 1 tablespoon fresh parsley, roughly chopped
- 1/4 cup fat-free feta cheese, crumbled

INSTRUCTIONS

1. Set the oven at 350° F (177° C) to preheat.
2. Grease 6 cups of the muffin tray with cooking spray.
3. Whisk eggs with salt, pepper and milk until foamy.
4. Add the remaining ingredients to the egg's mixture.
5. Divide the batter in the muffin cups equally.
6. Bake for 20 minutes until golden around the edges.
7. Serve warm.

NUTRITION FACTS

Servings: 2		
Amount per serving		
Calories		180
		% Daily Value*
Total Fat	6.4g	8%
Saturated Fat	1.6g	8%
Cholesterol	165mg	55%
Sodium	1341mg	58%
Total Carbohydrate	8.4g	3%
Dietary Fiber	1.3g	4%
Total Sugars	6g	
Protein	21.3g	
Vitamin D	16mcg	79%
Calcium	227mg	17%
Iron	2mg	10%
Potassium	351mg	

BAKED KALE AND EGGS WITH RICOTTA

Kale is a rich source of minerals; when added to an egg recipe it turns more nutritious than ever. That is why this baked egg combination with ricotta cheese is great to have kicking start in the morning.

Preparation Time: 10 Minutes	**Cooking Time:** 20 Minutes	**Allergens:** Eggs, Dairy

INGREDIENTS

- 6 cups kale, stems removed and chopped
- 1 tablespoon olive oil
- 2 cloves garlic, chopped
- 1/4 cup ricotta cheese, fat-free
- 1/4 cup feta, fat-free , crumbled
- 4 large eggs
- 1/3 cup grape tomatoes, cut in half
- 1/4 teaspoon ground black pepper
- 1/2 teaspoon Kosher salt

INSTRUCTIONS

1. Adjust the oven to 350° F (177° C).
2. Take a 9x13 inch casserole dish and grease it with cooking spray.
3. Warm a greased skillet on medium heat.
4. Stir in garlic and kale, sauté for 30 seconds until it is soft.
5. Transfer garlic mixture to a bowl and keep it aside.
6. Mix feta cheese and ricotta cheese in another bowl.
7. First spread the kale mixture in the casserole dish.
8. Make about 4 wells in the kale mixture and crack one egg into each well.
9. Spread cheese mixture on a top spoon by spoon.
10. Now spread the tomatoes over it and drizzle salt and pepper.
11. Bake for 20 minutes until golden brown.
12. Serve warm.

NUTRITION FACTS

Servings: 4		
Amount per serving		
Calories		202
		% Daily Value*
Total Fat	11.7g	15%
Saturated Fat	4.2g	21%
Cholesterol	199mg	66%
Sodium	529mg	23%
Total Carbohydrate	13.2g	5%
Dietary Fiber	1.7g	6%
Total Sugars	1.2g	
Protein	12.6g	
Vitamin D	18mcg	88%
Calcium	255mg	20%
Iron	3mg	15%
Potassium	629mg	13%

AVOCADO AND EGG BREAKFAST SANDWICH

Avocado sandwiches are always refreshing to serve as breakfast. These sandwiches, however, pair the delicious avocado spread with freshly baked eggs in a toasted bagel slice.

Preparation Time: 10 Minutes	**Cooking Time:** 5 Minutes	**Allergens:** Eggs

INGREDIENTS

- 1 whole wheat bagel
- 2 tablespoons olive oil
- 1 avocado, mashed
- 1 teaspoon lemon juice
- 2 eggs
- 1/4 teaspoon Kosher salt
- 1/4 teaspoon black pepper

NUTRITION FACTS

Servings: 4		
Amount per serving		
Calories		257
		% Daily Value*
Total Fat	19.4g	25%
Saturated Fat	3.8g	19%
Cholesterol	82mg	27%
Sodium	294mg	13%
Total Carbohydrate	16.9g	6%
Dietary Fiber	4.9g	18%
Total Sugars	2.7g	
Protein	6.5g	
Vitamin D	8mcg	39%
Calcium	56mg	4%
Iron	1mg	8%
Potassium	276mg	6%

INSTRUCTIONS

1. Slice the bagel in half to get two circles.
2. Scoop out some material from inside to make 1-inch wide hole in each half.
3. Brush the prepared slice with olive oil.
4. Sear these slices in a heated pan until golden brown from its sliced side.
5. Meanwhile, mix avocado flesh with lemon juice.
6. Spread the avocado mixture in the hole of the toasted bagel.
7. Crack an egg at the center of each slice and season it with salt and pepper.
8. Place them in the baking sheet. Bake for 4 minutes.
9. Serve warm.

BREAKFAST RECIPES

HAM, AND POACHED EGG ENGLISH MUFFIN

Bored with the traditional English muffins? Let's serve with something extra. Top the sliced muffins with ham, tomato, and a poached egg. That is how to make an ultra-Mediterranean breakfast in no time.

| **Preparation Time:** 10 Minutes | **Cooking Time:** 10 Minutes | **Allergens:** Eggs |

INGREDIENTS

- 1 tomato, cut into 4 slices
- 3 teaspoons olive oil
- 4 ham slices
- 2 whole wheat English muffins, halved
- 4 eggs, poached
- black pepper, to taste

INSTRUCTIONS

1. Warm 2 teaspoon olive oil in a skillet over medium heat.
2. Add ham and tomatoes, sauté until the ham turns golden in color.
3. Place the ham over the English muffin and then the softened tomatoes.
4. Top these muffins with poached eggs and drizzle olive oil on top.
5. Season it with black pepper.
6. Serve.

NUTRITION FACTS

Servings: 4		
Amount per serving		
Calories		257
		% Daily Value*
Total Fat	19.4g	25%
Saturated Fat	3.8g	19%
Cholesterol	82mg	27%
Sodium	294mg	13%
Total Carbohydrate	16.9g	6%
Dietary Fiber	4.9g	18%
Total Sugars	2.7g	
Protein	6.5g	
Vitamin D	8mcg	39%
Calcium	56mg	4%
Iron	1mg	8%
Potassium	276mg	6%

SMOOTHIE RECIPES

Mango smoothie

Beetroot smoothie

Avocado smoothie

Red smoothie

Green smoothie

Kale smoothie

Melon Smoothie

Pineapple smoothie

Kiwi smoothie

THE COMPLETE MEDITERRANEAN COOKBOOK 2019 EDITION

MANGO SMOOTHIE

Mangoes are famous for their sweet and soothing flavors and when it is combined with the refreshing twist of carrots and freshly squeezed orange juice. Garnish with mango cubes and carrot shred for a nice serving.

Preparation Time: 10 Minutes	**Cooking Time:** 0 Minutes	**Allergens:**

INGREDIENTS
- 2 cups of diced mango
- 1 carrot
- Juice from 1 orange
- Fresh mint leaves

INSTRUCTIONS
1. Add everything to a food processor.
2. Blend the ingredients well until smooth.
3. Refrigerate until chilled enough.
4. Serve with your favorite garnish
5. Enjoy.

NUTRITION FACTS

Servings: 1		
Amount per serving		
Calories		315
		% Daily Value*
Total Fat	1.6g	2%
Saturated Fat	0.4g	2%
Cholesterol	0mg	0%
Sodium	49mg	2%
Total Carbohydrate	78g	28%
Dietary Fiber	12g	43%
Total Sugars	65.3g	
Protein	5.3g	
Vitamin D	0mcg	39%
Calcium	153mg	12%
Iron	2mg	12%
Potassium	1135mg	24%

BEETROOT SMOOTHIE

Beetroot extracts are so full of nutrients and the antioxidants. When it is blended with lemon juice, carrot, pear, and apple, the resulting smoothie becomes so nutritious for our mind, skin and body.

| **Preparation Time:** 10 Minutes | **Cooking Time:** 0 Minutes | **Allergens:** |

INGREDIENTS
- 1 cup beetroot juice
- 2 teaspoons minced ginger
- 1 tablespoon lemon juice
- 1 apple, peeled, cored and diced
- 1 carrot, peeled and diced
- 1 pear, cored, peeled and diced

INSTRUCTIONS
1. Add everything to a food processor.
2. Blend the ingredients well until smooth.
3. Refrigerate until chilled enough.
4. Serve with your favorite garnish
5. Enjoy.

NUTRITION FACT

Servings: 1	
Amount per serving	
Calories	282
	% Daily Value*
Total Fat 1.1g	1%
Saturated Fat 0.2g	1%
Cholesterol 0mg	0%
Sodium 127mg	6%
Total Carbohydrate 70.8g	26%
Dietary Fiber 13.7g	49%
Total Sugars 48.2g	
Protein 3.7g	
Vitamin D 0mcg	0%
Calcium 55mg	4%
Iron 3mg	15%
Potassium 967mg	

AVOCADO SMOOTHIE

Those who fell for avocados every now and then will love to add this smoothie to their menu since it gives us the refreshing combination of avocado flesh blended with mint, linseeds, celery and lime juice.

| **Preparation Time:** 10 Minutes | **Cooking Time:** 0 Minutes | **Allergens:** |

INGREDIENTS

- ½ avocado pitted and peeled
- 3 celery stalks, chopped
- 1 lime, juiced
- Fresh mint leaves, chopped
- 1 tsp linseeds

INSTRUCTIONS

1. Add everything to a food processor.
2. Blend the ingredients well until smooth.
3. Refrigerate until chilled enough.
4. Serve with your favorite garnish
5. Enjoy.

NUTRITION FACTS

Servings: 1		
Amount per serving		
Calories		282
		% Daily Value*
Total Fat	22g	28%
Saturated Fat	4.4g	22%
Cholesterol	0mg	0%
Sodium	53mg	7%
Total Carbohydrate	19.6g	26%
Dietary Fiber	11.6g	41%
Total Sugars	2.4g	
Protein	4g	
Vitamin D	0mcg	0%
Calcium	90mg	7%
Iron	3mg	15%
Potassium	781mg	17%

RED SMOOTHIE

The name red smoothie comes from the color it was because of the raspberry in it. But this smoothie is the combination of raspberry with the blueberry along with plum. It is mainly flavored with lemon juice.

Preparation Time: 10 Minutes **Cooking Time:** 0 Minutes **Allergens:**

INGREDIENTS
- 4 plums, cored
- 3 tablespoons raspberry
- 3 tablespoons blueberry
- 1 tablespoon lemon juice
- 1 teaspoon linseed oil

INSTRUCTIONS
1. Add everything to a food processor.
2. Blend the ingredients well until smooth.
3. Refrigerate until chilled enough.
4. Serve with your favorite garnish
5. Enjoy.

NUTRITION FACTS

Servings: 1		
Amount per serving		
Calories		167
		% Daily Value*
Total Fat	1.2g	1%
Saturated Fat	0.1g	1%
Cholesterol	0mg	0%
Sodium	3mg	0%
Total Carbohydrate	39g	14%
Dietary Fiber	5.8g	21%
Total Sugars	32g	
Protein	2.6g	
Vitamin D	0mcg	0%
Calcium	7mg	1%
Iron	1mg	3%
Potassium	491mg	10%

GREEN SMOOTHIE

The green tells you that this smoothie is all about freshness. It is made out of blend spinach leaves with cucumber, lettuce, and parsley. To add more taste to it all, banana is added to the smoothie along with linseeds.

Preparation Time: 10 Minutes	**Cooking Time:** 0 Minutes	**Allergens:**

INGREDIENTS

- 2 cups of spinach leaves
- 1 cup of water
- 1 tablespoon of parsley
- 2 lettuce leaves
- 1 small cucumber, peeled and diced
- 1 banana, peeled
- 1 teaspoon of linseeds

INSTRUCTIONS

1. Add everything to a food processor.
2. Blend the ingredients well until smooth.
3. Refrigerate until chilled enough.
4. Serve with your favorite garnish
5. Enjoy.

NUTRITION FACTS

Servings: 1		
Amount per serving		
Calories		282
		% Daily Value*
Total Fat	1g	1%
Saturated Fat	0.3g	1%
Cholesterol	0mg	0%
Sodium	64mg	3%
Total Carbohydrate	40.6g	15%
Dietary Fiber	6.1g	22%
Total Sugars	19.8g	
Protein	5.1g	
Vitamin D	0mcg	0%
Calcium	126mg	10%
Iron	3mg	18%
Potassium	1237mg	26%

KALE SMOOTHIE

It's not all a kale smoothie. It is packed with the energy of the apple, banana and coconut milk. The drink is free from any processed sugars and only flavored using cinnamon ground which gives it a pleasing taste.

Preparation Time: 10 Minutes	**Cooking Time:** 0 Minutes	**Allergens:**

INGREDIENTS

- 2 cups of kale leaves
- 1 cup of coconut milk
- 1 banana
- 1 apple
- 1 teaspoon cinnamon

INSTRUCTIONS

1. Add everything to a food processor.
2. Blend the ingredients well until smooth.
3. Refrigerate until chilled enough.
4. Serve with your favorite garnish
5. Enjoy.

NUTRITION FACTS

Servings: 1		
Amount per serving		
Calories		287
		% Daily Value*
Total Fat	0.8g	1%
Saturated Fat	0.1g	1%
Cholesterol	0mg	0%
Sodium	61mg	3%
Total Carbohydrate	71.8g	26%
Dietary Fiber	10.5g	37%
Total Sugars	37.6g	
Protein	5.9g	
Vitamin D	0mcg	0%
Calcium	187mg	14%
Iron	3mg	19%
Potassium	1319mg	28%

MELON SMOOTHIE

Nothing can be as refreshing as the melon. To break the heat of the summer, this smoothie can be served as the best snack time drink. It is made out of melon, cucumber, mint, par and lemon juice.

| **Preparation Time:** 10 Minutes | **Cooking Time:** 0 Minutes | **Allergens:** |

INGREDIENTS
- ½ cucumber
- 2 slices of melon
- 2 Tsp lemon juice
- 1 pear
- 3 fresh mint leaves

INSTRUCTIONS
1. Add everything to a food processor.
2. Blend the ingredients well until smooth.
3. Refrigerate until chilled enough.
4. Serve with your favorite garnish
5. Enjoy.

NUTRITION FACTS

Servings: 1	
Amount per serving	
Calories	420
	% Daily Value*
Total Fat **2.4g**	3%
Saturated Fat **0.7g**	3%
Cholesterol **0mg**	0%
Sodium **158mg**	7%
Total Carbohydrate **101.7g**	37%
Dietary Fiber **15.4g**	55%
Total Sugars **85.6g**	
Protein **10.1g**	
Vitamin D **0mcg**	0%
Calcium **185mg**	14%
Iron **7mg**	37%
Potassium **2907mg**	62%

PINEAPPLE SMOOTHIE

Feel the breeze of the tropical winds with this refreshing pineapple smoothie. Bring strawberries, banana, pineapple, and orange juice together in a blender and make this super chilling pineapple smoothie for yourself.

Preparation Time: 10 Minutes	**Cooking Time:** 0 Minutes	**Allergens:**

INGREDIENTS

- ½ cup of fresh pineapple
- ½ cup of strawberry
- 1 banana
- ¼ cup of orange juice
- Mint ice cubes

INSTRUCTIONS

1. Add everything to a food processor.
2. Blend the ingredients well until smooth.
3. Refrigerate until chilled enough.
4. Serve with your favorite garnish
5. Enjoy.

NUTRITION FACTS

Servings: 1	
Amount per serving	
Calories	197
	% Daily Value*
Total Fat **0.8g**	1%
Saturated Fat **0.2g**	1%
Cholesterol **0mg**	0%
Sodium **3mg**	0%
Total Carbohydrate **49.8g**	18%
Dietary Fiber **5.8g**	21%
Total Sugars **31.3g**	
Protein **2.6g**	
Vitamin D **0mcg**	0%
Calcium **29mg**	2%
Iron **2mg**	9%
Potassium **747mg**	16%

KIWI SMOOTHIE

Surely you cannot miss out kiwi from your routine menu. Here is a way to add this delicious fruit to your diet. Make a refreshing smoothie out of it using pineapple, banana, and basil along with it.

| **Preparation Time:** 10 Minutes | **Cooking Time:** 0 Minutes | **Allergens:** |

INGREDIENTS
- 5 kiwis
- ½ cup of fresh pineapple
- 1 banana
- Basil leaves

INSTRUCTIONS
1. Add everything to a food processor.
2. Blend the ingredients well until smooth.
3. Refrigerate until chilled enough.
4. Serve with your favorite garnish
5. Enjoy.

NUTRITION FACTS

Servings: 1		
Amount per serving		
Calories		378
		% Daily Value*
Total Fat	2.5g	3%
Saturated Fat	0.3g	1%
Cholesterol	0mg	0%
Sodium	14mg	1%
Total Carbohydrate	93.5g	34%
Dietary Fiber	15.6g	56%
Total Sugars	56.7g	
Protein	6.1g	
Vitamin D	0mcg	0%
Calcium	147mg	11%
Iron	2mg	10%
Potassium	1700mg	36%

MEDITERRANEAN SMOOTHIE

This smoothie is the mother of all smoothies as it contains all the right ingredients to make it a super Mediterranean drink. It is a blended mixture of spinach, ginger, banana, mango, beet juice, and coconut milk.

Preparation Time: 10 Minutes	**Cooking Time:** 0 Minutes	**Allergens:**

INGREDIENTS

- 2 cups loosely packed baby spinach
- 1 teaspoon fresh ginger root, minced
- 1 frozen banana
- 1 small mango
- 1/2 cup beet juice
- 1/2 cup coconut milk
- 4-6 ice cubes

INSTRUCTIONS

1. Add everything to a food processor.
2. Blend the ingredients well until smooth.
3. Refrigerate until chilled enough.
4. Serve with your favorite garnish
5. Enjoy.

NUTRITION FACTS

Servings: 1	
Amount per serving	
Calories	528
	% Daily Value*
Total Fat 1.7g	2%
Saturated Fat 0.4g	2%
Cholesterol 2mg	1%
Sodium 432mg	19%
Total Carbohydrate 125.5g	46%
Dietary Fiber 18.5g	66%
Total Sugars 84.9g	
Protein 13.1g	
Vitamin D 1mcg	3%
Calcium 316mg	24%
Iron 10mg	56%
Potassium 1182mg	25%

COCONUT MILK SMOOTHIE

A sugar-free, mild and sweet coconut milk smoothie is a great addition to a healthy routine diet. Just blend in the milk with spinach and banana to get the full taste.

Preparation Time: 10 Minutes	**Cooking Time:** 0 Minutes	**Allergens:**

INGREDIENTS
- 1 1/2 cups coconut milk
- 1 frozen banana
- 2 cups raw baby spinach

INSTRUCTIONS
1. Add everything to a food processor.
2. Blend the ingredients well until smooth.
3. Refrigerate until chilled enough.
4. Serve with your favorite garnish
5. Enjoy.

NUTRITION FACTS

Servings: 1		
Amount per serving		
Calories		197
		% Daily Value*
Total Fat	14.6g	19%
Saturated Fat	12.8g	64%
Cholesterol	mg	0%
Sodium	33mg	1%
Total Carbohydrate	17.9g	7%
Dietary Fiber	3.5g	13%
Total Sugars	9.4g	
Protein	2.9g	
Vitamin D	0mcg	0%
Calcium	42mg	3%
Iron	2mg	11%
Potassium	536mg	11%

CREAMY STRAWBERRY SMOOTHIE

This one is rather a creamy and soothing mixture of all the refreshing fruits including mango, banana, and strawberries. Yogurt is used along with coconut milk to make the base of this smoothie thicker and richer in taste.

| **Preparation Time:** 10 Minutes | **Cooking Time:** 0 Minutes | **Allergens:** |

INGREDIENTS

- 1 banana
- 1/2 cup frozen strawberries
- 1/2 cup frozen mango
- 1/2 cup Greek yogurt
- 1/4 cup coconut milk
- 1/4 teaspoon turmeric
- 1/4 teaspoon ginger
- 1 Tablespoon honey

INSTRUCTIONS

1. Add everything to a food processor.
2. Blend the ingredients well until smooth.
3. Refrigerate until chilled enough.
4. Serve with your favorite garnish
5. Enjoy.

NUTRITION FACTS

Servings: 1		
Amount per serving		
Calories		545
		% Daily Value*
Total Fat	18.1g	23%
Saturated Fat	14.9g	75%
Cholesterol	20mg	7%
Sodium	112mg	5%
Total Carbohydrate	76.1g	28%
Dietary Fiber	7.4g	27%
Total Sugars	56.5g	
Protein	26.5g	
Vitamin D	0mcg	0%
Calcium	287mg	22%
Iron	2mg	12%
Potassium	950mg	20%

BLUEBERRY BANANA SMOOTHIE

There is no better detoxifier then fresh berries in your diet. that is why this smoothie is prepared entirely out blueberries blended with banana. To avoid any processed sugar, it is flavored with a small amount of honey.

| **Preparation Time:** 10 Minutes | **Cooking Time:** 0 Minutes | **Allergens:** Flaxseed meal |

INGREDIENTS

- 1 tablespoon flax seed meal
- 1 banana
- 1/2 cup frozen blueberries
- 1 tablespoon peanut butter
- 1 teaspoon honey
- 1/2 cup coconut yogurt
- 1 cup almond

INSTRUCTIONS

1. Add everything to a food processor.
2. Blend the ingredients well until smooth.
3. Refrigerate until chilled enough.
4. Serve with your favorite garnish
5. Enjoy.

NUTRITION FACTS

Servings: 1		
Amount per serving		
Calories		508
		% Daily Value*
Total Fat	17.4g	22%
Saturated Fat	6.4g	32%
Cholesterol	27mg	9%
Sodium	278mg	12%
Total Carbohydrate	69g	25%
Dietary Fiber	7.7g	27%
Total Sugars	48.6g	
Protein	22.1g	
Vitamin D	1mcg	6%
Calcium	524mg	40%
Iron	5mg	27%
Potassium	1069mg	23%

BASIC BREAKFAST SMOOTHIE

Can't cook the oatmeal bowl for your breakfast? Well, now you can make something better and quick with this fruit's oats smoothie. Simply the soaked oats are blended with banana and strawberries.

Preparation Time: 10 Minutes	**Cooking Time:** 0 Minutes	**Allergens:**

INGREDIENTS

- 3/4 cup coconut milk
- 1/4 cup old-fashioned oats
- 1 frozen banana
- 1 cup of frozen strawberries
- 2 tbsp Greek yogurt
- 1 tsp honey
- Dash of vanilla extract

INSTRUCTIONS

1. Soak oats in the milk in a blender. Let it sit for 10 minutes.
2. Add everything else to the blender.
3. Blend the ingredients well until smooth.
4. Refrigerate until chilled enough.
5. Serve with your favorite garnish
6. Enjoy.

NUTRITION FACTS

Servings: 1		
Amount per serving		
Calories		579
		% Daily Value*
Total Fat	5.5g	7%
Saturated Fat	2.6g	13%
Cholesterol	15mg	5%
Sodium	242mg	11%
Total Carbohydrate	84.8g	31%
Dietary Fiber	8.1g	29%
Total Sugars	54.1g	
Protein	52.3g	
Vitamin D	1mcg	5%
Calcium	725mg	56%
Iron	2mg	12%
Potassium	1169mg	25%

PINA COLADA SMOOTHIE

Pina cola is everyone's personal favorite, and so does this Pina colada smoothie which is made out of pineapple, mango and banana, all blended with the coconut milk and flaxseeds.

Preparation Time: 10 Minutes	**Cooking Time:** 0 Minutes	**Allergens:** Flaxseed

INGREDIENTS
- 1 banana
- ½ cup pineapple, peeled and sliced
- ½ cup mango, cored and diced
- 1/3 cup coconut milk
- ¼ cup ice
- 1 tablespoon flaxseed

INSTRUCTIONS
1. Add everything to a food processor.
2. Blend the ingredients well until smooth.
3. Refrigerate until chilled enough.
4. Serve with your favorite garnish
5. Enjoy.

NUTRITION FACTS

Servings: 1		
Amount per serving		
Calories		417
		% Daily Value*
Total Fat	22.1g	28%
Saturated Fat	17.4g	87%
Cholesterol	0mg	0%
Sodium	19mg	1%
Total Carbohydrate	56.6g	21%
Dietary Fiber	9.2g	33%
Total Sugars	36.6g	
Protein	5.5g	
Vitamin D	0mcg	0%
Calcium	42mg	3%
Iron	4mg	22%
Potassium	919mg	0%

POULTRY RECIPES

Mediterranean Chicken & Orzo

Chicken & White Bean Soup

Chicken with Tomato Sauce

Hasselback Caprese Chicken

Turkey Burgers with Feta & Tzatziki

Mediterranean Chicken Quinoa Bowl

Olive Chicken

Cheesy Chicken with Tomatoes

THE COMPLETE MEDITERRANEAN COOKBOOK 2019 EDITION

MEDITERRANEAN CHICKEN & ORZO

Let's infuse some different flavors to the slow cooked chicken with a special herb de Provence spice mixture. to make it a perfect weekday luncheon, pair the chicken with orzo and olives. With slow cooking, all the flavors are perfectly incorporated.

Preparation Time: 10 Minutes **Cooking Time:** 2 hours 30 minutes **Allergens:** Wheat

INGREDIENTS

- 1-pound boneless, skinless chicken breasts, trimmed
- 1 cup low-sodium chicken broth
- 2 medium tomatoes, chopped
- 1 medium onion, halved and sliced
- Zest and juice of 1 lemon
- 1 teaspoon herbs de Provence
- ½ teaspoon salt
- ½ teaspoon ground pepper
- ¾ cup whole-wheat orzo
- 1/3 cup quartered black or green olives
- 2 tablespoons chopped fresh parsley

NUTRITION FACTS

Servings: 4		
Amount per serving		
Calories		580
		% Daily Value*
Total Fat	22.4g	29%
Saturated Fat	3.7g	19%
Cholesterol	101mg	34%
Sodium	893mg	39%
Total Carbohydrate	46.7g	17%
Dietary Fiber	8.5g	30%
Total Sugars	3.8g	
Protein	47.9g	
Vitamin D	0mcg	0%
Calcium	34mg	3%
Iron	2mg	11%
Potassium	490mg	10%

INSTRUCTIONS

1. Slice each chicken breast into 4 equal sized pieces.
2. Add chicken, onion, tomatoes, lemon zest, juice, salt, pepper, herb de Provence and broth to a 6-quart slow cooker.
3. Cover the chicken mixture and cook on High settings for 2 hours.
4. Stir well and add orzo along with olives to the dish.
5. Let it cook for 30 minutes more on high settings.
6. Garnish with parsley and serve.
7. Enjoy.

CHICKEN & WHITE BEAN SOUP

A warming bowl of chicken soup can be your way to shake off of all the stress. Try making it with a leek, sage and white beans the soup will be turned into an energy boosting supplement for you and your family.

Preparation Time: 10 Minutes	**Cooking Time:** 15 minutes	**Allergens:** Absent

INGREDIENTS

- 2 teaspoons extra-virgin olive oil
- 2 leeks, cut into ¼-inch rounds
- 1 tablespoon chopped fresh sage,
- 2 (14-ounce) cans reduced-sodium chicken broth
- 2 cups of water
- 1 (15-ounce) can cannellini beans, rinsed
- 1 2-pound roasted chicken, skin discarded, meat removed from bones and shredded

NUTRITION FACTS

Servings: 4		
Amount per serving		
Calories		580
		% Daily Value*
Total Fat	12.9g	17%
Saturated Fat	3.2g	16%
Cholesterol	101mg	34%
Sodium	767mg	33%
Total Carbohydrate	71.2g	26%
Dietary Fiber	27.5g	98%
Total Sugars	4.7g	
Protein	62.6g	
Vitamin D	0mcg	0%
Calcium	215mg	17%
Iron	12mg	64%
Potassium	2028mg	43%

INSTRUCTIONS

1. Preheat a Dutch oven with oil on medium-high heat.
2. Stir in leeks and cook for 3 minutes then add sage.
3. Sauté for another 30 seconds and add water and broth.
4. Cook on high heat to bring it to a boil.
5. Stir in chicken and beans, cook for 3 minutes with occasional stirring.
6. Serve warm.

POULTRY RECIPES:

GREEK CHICKEN WITH ROASTED SPRING VEGETABLES

If the mix of the colorful roasted vegetables is not enough to make this dish sound appealing then consider the crusty seasoned chicken which is baked along with the veggies. The crispy and crunch of this recipe has no parallel.

Preparation Time: 10 Minutes	**Cooking Time:** 20 minutes	**Allergens:** wheat, egg, Dairy

INGREDIENTS

- 1 lemon
- 1 tablespoon olive oil
- 1 tablespoon crumbled feta cheese
- ½ teaspoon honey
- 2 (8 ounces) chicken breast, cut in half lengthwise
- ¼ cup light mayonnaise
- 6 cloves garlic, minced
- ½ cup panko bread crumbs
- 3 tablespoons grated Parmesan cheese
- ½ teaspoon kosher salt
- ½ teaspoon black pepper
- Nonstick olive oil cooking spray
- 2 cups 1-inch pieces asparagus
- 1½ cups sliced fresh cremini mushrooms
- 1½ cups chopped tomatoes
- 1 tablespoon olive oil
- Snipped fresh dill

INSTRUCTIONS

1. Place a 15 into 10 inches baking pan in the oven and preheat it over 4750 F (2460 C).
2. Flatten the chicken pieces with a mallet in a plastic wrap.
3. Now season them, with mayonnaise, and 2 garlic cloves.
4. Mix bread crumbs, with salt, pepper, and cheese in a bowl.
5. Dip the seasoned chicken into the crumbs mixture to coat well.
6. Shake off the excess and transfer the pieces to a greased baking sheet.
7. Bake them for 20 minutes. Flip the chicken half way through.
8. Saute remaining garlic with salt, pepper, and oil in a saucepan.
9. After cooking a minute at tomatoes, then cook for 5 minutes.
10. Stir in mushrooms, and asparagus.
11. Dice the baked chicken into bite size pieces.
12. Toss the chicken into the saucy asparagus.
13. Serve warm with desired garnishing.

NUTRITION FACTS

Servings: 4		
Amount per serving		
Calories		441
		% Daily Value*
Total Fat	20g	26%
Saturated Fat	7.3g	37%
Cholesterol	92mg	31%
Sodium	833mg	36%
Total Carbohydrate	26g	9%
Dietary Fiber	3.6g	13%
Total Sugars	7.4g	
Protein	41.5g	
Vitamin D	0mcg	0%
Calcium	215mg	26%
Iron	4mg	20%
Potassium	796mg	17%

CHICKEN WITH TOMATO SAUCE

The balsamic tomato sauce of this chicken recipe is the main specialty of it. the seared chicken is topped with a sauce made out of tomatoes, shallots, vinegar, and fennel seeds. Garnish with your favorite toppings.

| **Preparation Time:** 10 Minutes | **Cooking Time:** 15 minutes | **Allergens:** wheat, seeds |

INGREDIENTS

- 2 (8-ounce) boneless, skinless chicken breasts
- ½ teaspoon salt, divided
- ½ teaspoon ground pepper, divided
- ¼ cup white whole-wheat flour
- 3 tablespoons extra-virgin olive oil, divided
- ½ cup halved cherry tomatoes
- 2 tablespoons sliced shallot
- ¼ cup balsamic vinegar
- 1 cup low-sodium chicken broth
- 1 tablespoon minced garlic
- 1 tablespoon fennel seeds, toasted and lightly crushed
- 1 tablespoon butter

INSTRUCTIONS

1. Slice the chicken breasts horizontally into 4 equal sized pieces.
2. Cover the pieces with plastic sheet and pound them using a mallet into ¼ inch thickness.
3. Season them with salt and pepper.
4. Spread flour in shallow dish and dredge the chicken through it.
5. Shake off the excess flour once coated well.
6. Warm 2 tablespoons of cooking oil in a large skillet.
7. Add 2 pieces of chicken at a time to sear for 3 minutes per side.
8. Transfer this chicken to a plate and cover it with a foil.
9. Warm the remaining oil in the same pan and add tomatoes and shallot.
10. Stir cook for 2 minutes until soft then pour in the vinegar.
11. Let this mixture cook for 45 seconds then add broth, fennel seeds, salt, pepper, and garlic.
12. Cook for 5 mins until its sauce is reduced to half.
13. Add in butter and serve warm.

NUTRITION FACTS

Servings: 4		
Amount per serving		
Calories		304
		% Daily Value*
Total Fat	19.2g	25%
Saturated Fat	4.8g	24%
Cholesterol	73mg	24%
Sodium	107mg	5%
Total Carbohydrate	9.4g	3%
Dietary Fiber	1.7g	6%
Total Sugars	1.1g	
Protein	23.4g	
Vitamin D	2mcg	10%
Calcium	41mg	3%
Iron	2mg	10%
Potassium	270mg	6%

POULTRY RECIPES:

SOUVLAKI KEBABS WITH VEGETABLE COUSCOUS

These kebabs are famous for their unique appearance and juicy taste. And when they are served with couscous salad, it tastes even more delectable. The kebabs are marinated and then grilled until al dente.

| **Preparation Time:** 10 Minutes | **Cooking Time:** 10 minutes | **Allergens:** Absent |

INGREDIENTS

- 1-pound skinless, boneless chicken breast halves, cut into ½-inch strips
- 1 cup sliced fennel
- 1/3 cup dry white wine
- ¼ cup lemon juice
- 3 tablespoons canola oil
- 4 cloves garlic, minced
- 2 teaspoons dried oregano, crushed
- ½ teaspoon salt
- ¼ teaspoon black pepper
- 1 teaspoon olive oil
- ½ cup Israeli (large pearl) couscous
- 1 cup of water
- ½ cup snipped dried tomatoes
- ¾ cup chopped red sweet pepper
- ½ cup chopped cucumber
- ½ cup chopped red onion
- 1/3 cup plain fat-free Greek yogurt
- ¼ cup thinly sliced fresh basil leaves
- ¼ cup snipped fresh parsley
- 1 tablespoon lemon juice
- ¼ teaspoon salt
- ¼ teaspoon black pepper

INSTRUCTIONS

1. Combine lemon juice with white wine, garlic, salt, pepper, oregano, and oil.
2. Reserve 1/4th of the marinade and pour the remaining in a plastic bag.
3. Add chicken and fennel to the same bag. Seal and shake it to coat well.
4. Refrigerate this bag for 1 ½ hour at least for marination.
5. Soak wooden skewers in water for 30 minutes then drain and dry them.
6. Remove the chicken from its marinade then discard the fennel.
7. Thread the chicken onto the skewers in accordion style.
8. Preheat the grill on medium-high heat.
9. Grill the chicken for 4 minutes per side.
10. Brush the skewers with the reserved marinade during grilling.
11. Warm 1 teaspoon olive oil on medium heat in a saucepan.
12. Stir in ½ cup couscous and stir cook for 4 minutes.
13. Add a cup of water and cook until it boils.
14. Cook for 10 minutes then add tomatoes.
15. Toss the couscous with red onion, sweet pepper, cucumber, yogurt, parsley, lemon juice, salt, and pepper.
16. Serve the kabobs with prepared couscous and fennel leaves.

NUTRITION FACTS

Servings: 4		
Amount per serving		
Calories		326
		% Daily Value*
Total Fat	16.2g	21%
Saturated Fat	2.6g	13%
Cholesterol	66mg	22%
Sodium	355mg	15%
Total Carbohydrate	13.6g	5%
Dietary Fiber	2.5g	9%
Total Sugars	3.4g	
Protein	28.4g	
Vitamin D	0mcg	0%
Calcium	53mg	4%
Iron	2mg	11%
Potassium	327mg	7%

POULTRY RECIPES:

HASSELBACK CAPRESE CHICKEN

It has a load of protein and fats in a single serving. the chicken is first sliced and then filled with caprese and tomatoes. When it is all baked together, you can see a pattern of appealing colors and taste juices coming out of the chicken fillets.

| **Preparation Time:** 10 Minutes | **Cooking Time:** 25 minutes | **Allergens:** Absent |

INGREDIENTS
- 1 cup frozen chopped spinach, thawed
- 1 pound 93% lean ground turkey
- ½ cup crumbled feta cheese
- ½ teaspoon garlic powder
- ½ teaspoon dried oregano
- ¼ teaspoon salt
- ¼ teaspoon ground pepper
- 4 small hamburger buns, preferably whole-wheat, split
- 4 tablespoons tzatziki
- 12 slices cucumber
- 8 thick rings red onion (about ¼-inch)
- Tomato slices

INSTRUCTIONS

1. Preheat the grill on medium-high heat.
2. Squeeze the liquid out of the spinach.
3. Toss this spinach with feta, minced turkey, salt, pepper, oregano and garlic powder in a bowl.
4. Mix well and prepare for small patties out of this mixture.
5. Grease the grilling grates and place the patties in the grill.
6. Cook for 6 minutes per side.
7. Place the cooked each patty in the buns with cucumber slices, tomato slices, onion rings, tzatziki.
8. Serve warm.

NUTRITION FACTS

Servings: 4		
Amount per serving		
Calories		309
		% Daily Value*
Total Fat	15.6g	20%
Saturated Fat	4.6g	23%
Cholesterol	101mg	34%
Sodium	502mg	22%
Total Carbohydrate	2.4g	1%
Dietary Fiber	0.4g	2%
Total Sugars	0.8g	
Protein	38.9g	
Vitamin D	0mcg	0%
Calcium	23mg	2%
Iron	6mg	34%
Potassium	350mg	7%

POULTRY RECIPES:

TURKEY BURGERS WITH FETA & TZATZIKI

Burgers are a sure thing when it comes to any cuisine. These burgers are made out of turkey mince and spinach along with spices. Once the patties are grilled, they are serving with vegetable sliced and the whole wheat bun.

| **Preparation Time:** 10 Minutes | **Cooking Time:** 15 minutes | **Allergens:** wheat |

INGREDIENTS

- 2 boneless, skinless chicken breasts
- ½ teaspoon salt, divided
- ½ teaspoon ground pepper, divided
- 1 medium tomato, sliced
- 3 ounces fresh mozzarella, halved and sliced
- ¼ cup prepared pesto
- 8 cups broccoli florets
- 2 tablespoons extra-virgin olive oil

INSTRUCTIONS

1. Set the oven at 375º F (190º C) to preheat.
2. Later a baking sheet with cooking spray.
3. Carve 3 to 4 -½ inch long crosswise cuts over the chicken breasts.
4. Season the chicken with salt and pepper.
5. Insert tomato and mozzarella slices in the chicken cuts.
6. Brush it with pesto on top.
7. Place the chicken breasts in the baking sheet.
8. Toss broccoli with oil, salt, and pepper in a large bowl.
9. Spread the broccoli mixture around the chicken.
10. Bake it for 25 minutes.
11. Serve warm.

NUTRITION FACTS

Servings: 4		
Amount per serving		
Calories		508
		% Daily Value*
Total Fat	16.9g	22%
Saturated Fat	6.1g	31%
Cholesterol	104mg	35%
Sodium	738mg	32%
Total Carbohydrate	60.5g	22%
Dietary Fiber	6.2g	22%
Total Sugars	20.9g	
Protein	34.7g	
Vitamin D	0mcg	0%
Calcium	358mg	28%
Iron	6mg	33%
Potassium	1430mg	30%

MEDITERRANEAN CHICKEN QUINOA BOWL

A light and healthy meal for everyone struggling against obesity or weight gain. It offers a complete set of nutrients with more proteins and fibers. the baked chicken is shredded and added to the colorful quinoa mixture.

Preparation Time: 10 Minutes	**Cooking Time:** 15 minutes	**Allergens:** Nuts, Dairy

INGREDIENTS

- 1-pound boneless, skinless chicken breasts, trimmed
- ¼ teaspoon salt
- ¼ teaspoon ground pepper
- 1 (7-ounce) jar roasted red peppers, rinsed
- ¼ cup slivered almonds
- 4 tablespoons extra-virgin olive oil, divided
- 1 small clove garlic, crushed
- 1 teaspoon paprika
- ½ teaspoon ground cumin
- ¼ teaspoon crushed red pepper (optional)
- 2 cups cooked quinoa
- ¼ cup pitted Kalamata olives, chopped
- ¼ cup finely chopped red onion
- 1 cup diced cucumber
- ¼ cup crumbled feta cheese
- 2 tablespoons finely chopped fresh parsley

INSTRUCTIONS

1. Place the oven rack in the upper portion of the oven.
2. Preheat the oven on broiler setting.
3. Layer a baking sheet with foil and set it aside.
4. Season the chicken with salt and pepper.
5. Place it on the baking sheet and broil it for 15 minutes.
6. Once done, allow the chicken to cool for 5 minutes then transfer it to a cutting board.
7. Slice and shred the chicken.
8. Blend almonds, pepper, paprika, garlic, 1 tablespoon oil, cumin and red pepper in a blender.
9. Toss quinoa with red onion, 2 tablespoon oil, olives and quinoa in a bowl.
10. Divide the quinoa mixture in the serving bowls and top it with cucumber, shredded chicken and red pepper sauce.
11. Garnish with parsley and feta.
12. Serve.

NUTRITION FACTS

Servings: 4	
Amount per serving	
Calories	741
	% Daily Value*
Total Fat 33.7g	43%
Saturated Fat 6.7g	33%
Cholesterol 109mg	36%
Sodium 548mg	24%
Total Carbohydrate 62.1g	23%
Dietary Fiber 8.2g	29%
Total Sugars 3.6g	
Protein 48.4g	
Vitamin D 0mcg	0%
Calcium 144mg	11%
Iron 7mg	37%
Potassium 967mg	21%

POULTRY RECIPES:

CHICKEN & SPINACH SOUP WITH FRESH PESTO

Pesto has this distinct basil taste which rightly complements the basic flavor of this chicken and spinach soup. first, the soup is cooked through simmer, and when done it is mixed pesto for seasoning.

| **Preparation Time:** 10 Minutes | **Cooking Time:** 10 minutes | **Allergens:** wheat, Dairy |

INGREDIENTS

- 2 teaspoons 1 tablespoon extra-virgin olive oil
- ½ cup carrot, diced
- 1 large boneless, chicken breast, cut into 4 pieces
- 1 large clove garlic, minced
- 5 cups chicken broth or stock
- 1½ teaspoons marjoram, dried
- 6 ounces baby spinach, chopped coarsely
- 1 (15-ounce) can cannellini beans, rinsed
- ¼ cup grated Parmesan cheese
- 1/3 cup lightly packed fresh basil leaves
- Freshly ground pepper to taste
- ¾ cup plain or herbed multigrain croutons

INSTRUCTIONS

1. Grease a Dutch oven with 2 teaspoons oil and heat it.
2. Stir in carrot and chicken. Cook for the chicken for 4 minutes per side.
3. Add garlic and sauté for 1 minute.
4. Stir in marjoram and broth. Let it cook to a boil.
5. Reduce the heat of the broth down to a simmer for 5 minutes.
6. Transfer the chicken to a cutting board with a slotted spoon.
7. Add beans and spinach to the soup. Cook for another 5 minutes.
8. Blend parmesan, basil, and oil to a blender until smooth.
9. Dice the chicken into bite-sized pieces and add them to the soup.
10. Stir basil pesto and adjust seasoning with pepper.
11. Garnish with croutons.
12. Serve.

NUTRITION FACTS

Servings: 4	
Amount per serving	
Calories	597
	% Daily Value*
Total Fat 8.7g	11%
Saturated Fat 1.3g	7%
Cholesterol 73mg	24%
Sodium 1136mg	49%
Total Carbohydrate 72.8g	26%
Dietary Fiber 28.4g	101%
Total Sugars 4.1g	
Protein 57.6g	
Vitamin D 0mcg	0%
Calcium 254mg	20%
Iron 12mg	66%
Potassium 2471mg	53%

MEDITERRANEAN CHICKEN WITH POTATOES

This chicken vegetable combination is hard to resist for everyone. It is made out of juicy chicken and pan-cooked vegetables which mainly included the red potatoes, olives and artichoke hearts.

Preparation Time: 10 Minutes	**Cooking Time:** 40 minutes	**Allergens:** Dairy

INGREDIENTS

- 4 teaspoons minced garlic, divided
- 1 tablespoon olive oil
- 1 teaspoon salt, divided
- 1/4 teaspoon dried thyme
- 1/2 teaspoon black pepper, divided
- 12 small red potatoes, halved (about 1 1/2 pounds)
- Cooking spray
- 2 pounds chicken breast, cut into bite-sized pieces
- 1 cup red onion, sliced
- 3/4 cup dry white wine
- 3/4 cup chicken broth
- 1/2 cup chopped pepperoncini peppers
- 1/4 cup pitted kalamata olives, halved
- 2 cups chopped plum tomato
- 2 tablespoons chopped fresh basil
- 1 (14-ounce) can artichoke hearts, quartered
- 1/2 cup (2 ounces) grated fresh Parmesan cheese
- Thyme sprigs (optional)

INSTRUCTIONS

1. Set the oven at 400° F (200° C) to preheat.
2. Toss salt, garlic, oil, thyme, potatoes, and black pepper.
3. Spread them in a baking sheet and bake for 30 minutes at 400o F (204o C).
4. Grease a Dutch oven with cooking spray and warm it over medium heat.
5. Season the chicken with salt and pepper.
6. Sear this chicken for 5 minutes per side.
7. Cook the chicken in two batches. Transfer the chicken to a plate.
8. Add onion to the same pan for 5 minutes.
9. Stir in wine and deglaze the pan. Cook the mixture until reduced to 1/3 cup.
10. Add chicken, broth, potatoes, olives, and pepperoncini.
11. Sauté for 3 minutes then add garlic, salt, basil, artichokes, tomatoes.
12. Cook for another 3 minutes.
13. Garnish with thyme sprigs and cheese.
14. Serve.

NUTRITION FACTS

Servings: 6	
Amount per serving	
Calories	534
	% Daily Value*
Total Fat 9.1g	12%
Saturated Fat 2.6g	13%
Cholesterol 88mg	29%
Sodium 701mg	30%
Total Carbohydrate 66.8g	24%
Dietary Fiber 10.4g	37%
Total Sugars 6.3g	
Protein 43.8g	
Vitamin D 0mcg	0%
Calcium 89mg	7%
Iron 5mg	28%
Potassium 1888mg	40%

POULTRY RECIPES:

OLIVE CHICKEN

There are not many vegetables added to chicken in this recipe; it is an aromatic blend of chicken juices and tomatoes mixed sauce in which the chicken cooked. Once done it is then topped with the olives to serve and enjoy.

Preparation Time: 10 Minutes　　**Cooking Time:** 35 minutes　　**Allergens:** Absent

INGREDIENTS

- 2 teaspoons olive oil
- 2 tablespoons white wine
- 6 skinless, boneless chicken breast halves
- 3 cloves garlic, minced
- 1/2 cup diced onion
- 3 cups tomatoes, chopped
- 1/2 cup white wine
- 2 teaspoons chopped fresh thyme
- 1 tablespoon chopped fresh basil
- 1/2 cup kalamata olives
- 2 fennel bulbs, sliced in half
- 1/4 cup chopped fresh parsley
- salt and pepper to taste

INSTRUCTIONS

1. warm oil with 2 tablespoons white wine in a large skillet on medium heat.
2. Add chicken and cook for 6 minutes per side.
3. Transfer the chicken to a plate.
4. Stir in garlic then sauté for 30 seconds.
5. Add onion to sauté for 3 minutes.
6. Stir in fennel, tomatoes and let it boil.
7. Reduce the heat then add half cup white wine. Cook for 10 minutes.
8. Stir in basil and thyme, cook for 5 minutes.
9. Return the cooked chicken to the skillet.
10. Cover the cooking pan and cook on low heat under chicken is all done.
11. Stir parsley and olives.
12. Cook for 1 minute and adjust seasoning with salt and pepper.
13. Serve warm.

NUTRITION FACTS

Servings: 6	
Amount per serving	
Calories	428
	% Daily Value*
Total Fat 13.7g	18%
Saturated Fat 4.4g	22%
Cholesterol 173mg	58%
Sodium 211mg	9%
Total Carbohydrate 6.1g	2%
Dietary Fiber 1.9g	7%
Total Sugars 2.9g	
Protein 67.9g	
Vitamin D 0mcg	0%
Calcium 35mg	3%
Iron 3mg	18%
Potassium 257mg	

POULTRY RECIPES:

CHEESY CHICKEN WITH TOMATOES

This chicken recipe is mostly used to serve the pasta with. Its cheese content and creamy texture make it perfect to top your boiled penne pasta. Make sure to use the whole wheat pasta for best taste and nutrients.

| **Preparation Time:** 10 Minutes | **Cooking Time:** 15 minutes | **Allergens:** Wheat, Dairy |

INGREDIENTS
- 4 chicken breasts
- 2 tbsp minced garlic or garlic paste
- Salt and pepper, to taste
- 1 tbsp dried oregano, divided
- 1/2 cup dry white wine
- 1 large lemon, juice of
- 1/2 cup chicken broth
- 1 cup finely chopped red onion
- 1 1/2 cup small diced tomatoes
- 1/4 cup sliced green olives
- A handful of fresh parsley stems removed, chopped
- Crumbled feta cheese, optional

INSTRUCTIONS

1. Carve three slits over the chicken breasts on each of its sides.
2. Rub both the sides with garlic and insert them into the slits.
3. Season the chicken with oregano, salt, and pepper.
4. Warm an iron skillet with 2 tablespoons olive oil on medium heat.
5. Sear the chicken from both sides.
6. Stir in white wine, lemon juice, and broth.
7. Reduce the heat then cover the chicken then cook for 10 minutes.
8. Remove the lid then add olives, tomatoes, and onions.
9. Cook for 3 minutes, then garnish with feta cheese and parsley.
10. Serve warm with pasta.

NUTRITION FACTS

Servings: 4		
Amount per serving		
Calories		309
		% Daily Value*
Total Fat	4.4g	6%
Saturated Fat	0.2g	1%
Cholesterol	130mg	43%
Sodium	365mg	16%
Total Carbohydrate	8.1g	3%
Dietary Fiber	2.2g	8%
Total Sugars	3.4g	
Protein	54.1g	
Vitamin D	0mcg	0%
Calcium	52mg	4%
Iron	3mg	16%
Potassium	359mg	8%

POULTRY RECIPES:

ROASTED MEDITERRANEAN CHICKEN

Roasted chicken always sounds delicious when you plan a festive dinner. And when you get to serve it with mushrooms, asparagus, beans, and lots of dried herbs and spices, the deal becomes irresistible.

Preparation Time: 10 Minutes **Cooking Time:** 45 minutes **Allergens:** Absent

INGREDIENTS
- 2 tablespoons fresh parsley, chopped
- 1 tablespoon fresh oregano
- 1 tablespoon fresh basil, chopped
- ¼ teaspoon salt
- 1 teaspoon fresh rosemary, chopped
- ¼ teaspoon black pepper, ground
- 1½ lbs. chicken thighs, boneless and skinless
- 8 oz. mushrooms, diced
- 1 red onion, sliced
- ½ cup chopped red and/or green bell pepper
- 2 cloves garlic, minced
- 1 tablespoon olive oil
- 1-pound asparagus spears, trimmed and cut
- 1 (16 ounce) can cannellini beans
- 1 cup cherry tomatoes, diced
- 10 pitted kalamata olives, sliced
- 2 tablespoons balsamic vinegar

INSTRUCTIONS

1. Adjust the oven at 425o F (218o C) to preheat.
2. Layer 2 15x10 inch baking pan with tin foil. Keep them aside.
3. Combine oregano, rosemary, basil, salt, pepper and parsley in a bowl.
4. Place the chicken in the pans and season it with herbs mixture liberally.
5. Toss mushrooms with bell pepper, garlic, onion, and oil.
6. Add this mixture to the pan around the chicken.
7. Roast them for 30 minutes and continue tossing them after 10 minutes.
8. Add beans, asparagus, tomatoes, olives and balsamic vinegar and basil mixture to the chicken pans.
9. Bake again for 15 minutes.
10. Serve warm.

NUTRITION FACTS

Servings: 4		
Amount per serving		
Calories		498
		% Daily Value*
Total Fat	8.6g	11%
Saturated Fat	0.6g	3%
Cholesterol	109mg	36%
Sodium	497mg	22%
Total Carbohydrate	52.7g	19%
Dietary Fiber	19.3g	69%
Total Sugars	4.4g	
Protein	54.1g	
Vitamin D	204mcg	1021%
Calcium	186mg	14%
Iron	9mg	53%
Potassium	1889mg	40%

POULTRY RECIPES:

CHICKEN & WINTER SQUASH

There are not many recipes which you can make that easily using a squash. But this one with chicken and dried herbs plus spices is not only quick to make, but it is also super delicious.

Preparation Time: 10 Minutes	**Cooking Time:** 25 minutes	**Allergens:** Seeds, Dairy

INGREDIENTS

- 2½ pounds acorn squash
- 3 tablespoons extra-virgin olive oil, divided
- 2 tablespoons whole-grain mustard, divided
- 3 cloves garlic, minced
- 1 tablespoon chopped fresh rosemary
- 1 teaspoon grated lemon zest
- 2 tablespoons lemon juice, divided
- 1 teaspoon ground pepper, divided
- ½ teaspoon salt, divided
- 1-pound boneless, skinless chicken breast
- 1 tablespoon pure maple syrup
- 1½ teaspoons fresh thyme leaves
- 8 cups mixed salad greens
- 4 teaspoons grated Parmesan cheese
- 4 teaspoons salted roasted pumpkin seeds

INSTRUCTIONS

1. Set the oven at 425° F (218° C) to preheat.
2. Line a baking sheet with cooking spray.
3. Slice the squash lengthwise and remove its seeds.
4. Dice the flesh into 1-inch slices.
5. Mix 1 tbsp oil, mustard, rosemary, garlic, lemon juice and zest, pepper, and salt in a bowl.
6. Stir in chicken and sliced squash. Mix well to coat all the pieces.
7. Spread them in a baking sheet in a single layer.
8. Bake them for 22 minutes until golden brown.
9. Transfer the chicken to cutting board and dice it.
10. Combine 2 tablespoon oil, ½ tablespoon mustard, thyme, pepper, salt, maple syrup and 1 ½ tablespoons lemon juice in a separate bowl.
11. Toss in greens and mix well to coat.
12. Divide the seasoned greens in the serving plates, top them with an equal amount of chicken and squash.
13. Garnish with parmesan and pumpkin seeds.
14. Serve warm.

NUTRITION FACTS

Servings: 4	
Amount per serving	
Calories	794
	% Daily Value*
Total Fat 16.8g	22%
Saturated Fat 3g	15%
Cholesterol 78mg	26%
Sodium 559mg	24%
Total Carbohydrate 139.9g	51%
Dietary Fiber 19g	68%
Total Sugars 3.2g	
Protein 39.7g	
Vitamin D 0mcg	0%
Calcium 545mg	42%
Iron 13mg	71%
Potassium 5084mg	108%

POULTRY RECIPES:

LEMON-THYME CHICKEN

It is a nice party meal which is loved by all for its potato fingerlings. they are baked with seasoned chicken. The lemon thyme chicken is actually seared in the pan once it is completely flavored with spices and lemon juice.

Preparation Time: 10 Minutes   **Cooking Time:** 20 minutes   **Allergens:** Absent

INGREDIENTS

- 4 teaspoons extra-virgin olive oil, divided
- 1 teaspoon crushed dried thyme, divided
- ½ teaspoon kosher salt
- ¼ teaspoon freshly ground black pepper
- 1-pound fingerling potatoes halved lengthwise
- 4 small skinless, boneless chicken breast halves
- 2 cloves garlic, minced
- 1 lemon, thinly sliced

INSTRUCTIONS

1. Warm 2 teaspoons of oil in a skillet over medium heat.
2. Add ½ teaspoon thyme, pepper, salt, and potatoes.
3. Stir cook for a minute then cover it and cook for 12 minutes with occasional stirring.
4. Push the potatoes to a side then add remaining oil and place chicken in it.
5. Sear the chicken pieces for 5 minutes per side.
6. Sprinkle each side ½ teaspoon thyme.
7. Place lemon slices over the chicken and again cover the pan.
8. Cook for 10 minutes until chicken is done.
9. Serve warm.

NUTRITION FACTS

Servings: 4		
Amount per serving		
Calories		483
		% Daily Value*
Total Fat	9.4g	12%
Saturated Fat	0.7g	4%
Cholesterol	195mg	65%
Sodium	523mg	23%
Total Carbohydrate	18.8g	7%
Dietary Fiber	2.1g	7%
Total Sugars	1.2g	
Protein	80.3g	
Vitamin D	0mcg	0%
Calcium	20mg	2%
Iron	3mg	19%
Potassium	526mg	11%

BEEF, PORK AND LAMB RECIPES

Pork Tenderloin with Orzo

Pork Chops

Mediterranean Pork Medallions

Blue Cheese-Topped Pork Chops

Roasted Pepper Meat Loaf

Herbed Beef Skewers

Vegetables Lamb Shanks

Grilled London Broil

Lamb Pasta & Cheese

Spinach Beef Pinwheels

THE COMPLETE MEDITERRANEAN COOKBOOK 2019 EDITION

PORK TENDERLOIN WITH ORZO

BEEF, PORK AND LAMB RECIPES

When seared tenderloin is served with nicely cooked orzo pasta, it makes this recipe irresistible for all. The orzo is cooked with spinach, tomatoes, and feta cheese; then the pork is stirred in.

Preparation time: 5 minutes	**Cooking time:** 10 minutes	**Allergens:** Dairy

INGREDIENTS:

- 1-1/2 pounds pork tenderloin
- 1 teaspoon coarsely ground pepper
- 2 tablespoons olive oil
- 3 quarts water
- 1-1/4 cups uncooked orzo pasta
- 1/4 teaspoon salt
- 1 package (6 ounces) fresh baby spinach
- 1 cup grape tomatoes, halved
- 3/4 cup crumbled feta cheese

INSTRUCTIONS:

1. Dice the pork into cubes after seasoning it with pepper.
2. Take a skillet and preheat oil in it on medium heat.
3. Toss in the pork cubes and sear them for 10 minutes until they turn brown in color.
4. Meanwhile, Let the water to a boil in a Dutch oven.
5. Add salt along with orzo and let it cook for 8 minutes.
6. Stir in spinach and cook the orzo for 1 minute more, then drain it.
7. Toss tomatoes, pork, feta cheese, and rest of the ingredients.
8. Add the drained orzo and mix gently.
9. Serve warm.

NUTRITION FACTS

Serving 4		
Amount per serving		
Calories		683
		% Daily Value*
Total Fat	20.2g	26%
Saturated Fat	7g	35%
Cholesterol	201mg	67%
Sodium	616mg	27%
Total Carbohydrate	74.5g	27%
Dietary Fiber	1.5g	5%
Total Sugars	2.5g	
Protein	49.8g	
Vitamin D	0mcg	0%
Calcium	233mg	18%
Iron	7mg	39%
Potassium	1075mg	23%

THE COMPLETE MEDITERRANEAN COOKBOOK 2019 EDITION

PORK CHOPS

Seasoned pork chops are seared and then cooked in a saucy mixture with tomatoes and olives, that is why the chops are full of crispy and the juicy taste. further, the saucy mix is served feta cheese and parsley on top.

| **Preparation Time:** 05 Minutes | **Cooking Time:** 20 minutes | **Allergens:** Dairy |

INGREDIENTS
- 1 lb thin boneless pork loin chop
- cooking spray, to coat
- garlic salt, to taste
- ground black pepper, to taste sauce
- 1 teaspoon olive oil
- 1 cup red onion, chopped
- 2 garlic cloves, minced
- 1 lemon, juice of
- 1 tablespoon balsamic vinegar
- 1 tablespoon whole grain dijon mustard
- ¼ teaspoon sea salt
- ¼ teaspoon ground black pepper
- ½ teaspoon dried oregano
- 2 (1 ounce) packets splenda
- 2 tablespoons capers
- 8 ounces grape tomatoes, whole
- ½ cup pitted kalamata olive, whole

TOPPINGS
- 2 tablespoons fresh parsley, chopped to top
- feta cheese, to the top (optional)

INSTRUCTIONS

1. Coat the pork chops with oil, garlic salt, and pepper liberally.
2. Use either grill or oven to cook the chops.
3. Preheat the oven for baking up to 375o F (190o C).
4. Bake the chops in the preheated oven until it cooked from both the sides.
5. During this time, pour oil in a skillet and heat it.
6. Toss in onion and saute it for 5 mins then add garlic.
7. Stir cook for 2 mins then add rest of the ingredients.
8. Continue sauteing for 5 minutes more.
9. Pour this mixture over the baked chops.
10. Garnish with feta and parsley.
11. Enjoy.

NUTRITION FACTS

Servings: 4		
Amount per serving		
Calories		734
		% Daily Value*
Total Fat	36.9g	47%
Saturated Fat	10.9g	55%
Cholesterol	151mg	50%
Sodium	1092mg	47%
Total Carbohydrate	44.8g	16%
Dietary Fiber	5.1g	18%
Total Sugars	34.6g	
Protein	44.9g	
Vitamin D	0mcg	0%
Calcium	78mg	6%
Iron	4mg	25%
Potassium	426mg	9%

GARLIC AND ROSEMARY MEDITERRANEAN PORK ROAST

BEEF, PORK AND LAMB RECIPES

Rosemary pork roast is famous for its mild and earthy flavors. The pork roast is seasoned with dried rosemary herbs, black pepper and salt liberally. The roast is cooked first in the skillet and then baked in the oven.

Preparation time: 5 minutes	**Cooking time:** 35 minutes	**Allergens:**

NUTRITION FACTS

Serving 6		
Amount per serving		
Calories		363
		% Daily Value*
Total Fat	18.7g	24%
Saturated Fat	5.7g	28%
Cholesterol	150mg	50%
Sodium	498mg	22%
Total Carbohydrate	0.6g	0%
Dietary Fiber	0.1g	0%
Total Sugars	0g	
Protein	46.1g	
Vitamin D	0mcg	0%
Calcium	44mg	3%
Iron	2mg	12%
Potassium	8mg	0%

INGREDIENTS

- 2 to 2 and 1/2 lb. pork sirloin roast
- 3 garlic cloves, sliced lengthwise into slivers
- Leaves of one sprig of fresh rosemary (about 3 dozen leaves)
- 1 teaspoon salt
- 1/2 teaspoon black pepper
- 2 tablespoon olive oil

INSTRUCTIONS

1. Let your oven preheat at 250° F (121° C).
2. Carve 12 deep slits over the pork roasts using a sharp knife.
3. Stuff these slits with rosemary and garlic slivers.
4. Drizzle salt and pepper on top and season the roast liberally.
5. Take a suitable skillet and preheat oil in it.
6. Place roast in the skillet and cook it until brown from both the sides.
7. Transfer this roast pan to the preheated oven and bake it for 70 minutes.
8. Flip the roast after 35 minutes of baking.
9. Slice and serve with salad.

MEDITERRANEAN PORK MEDALLIONS

Both the rice and the pork is cooked in the vinaigrette dressing which infuses great taste into the recipe. once the rice is cooked with tomatoes and green beans, the pork cooked in a quarter of the dressing is served on top of them.

Preparation time: 5 minutes	**Cooking time:** 30 minutes	**Allergens:** Dairy

INGREDIENTS

- 1/2 cup Sun Dried Tomato
- ½ cup Vinaigrette Dressing
- 1 cup frozen cut green beans
- 1 can (14 oz.) fat-free reduced-sodium chicken broth
- 2 cups instant white rice, uncooked
- 1 pork tenderloin (1 lb.), cut crosswise into 8 slices
- 1 teaspoon dried rosemary leaves, crushed
- 1 cup chopped plum tomatoes
- 2 Tablespoon Grated Parmesan Cheese

INSTRUCTIONS

1. Take a saucepan and heat ¼ cup of the vinaigrette dressing in it.
2. Once heat, add the bean to a cook for 1 minute.
3. Pour in broth and heat it to a boil then cook it for 3 minutes on a simmer.
4. Stir in rice and cook for 5 minutes more on a simmer.
5. On the other hand, pound the pork with a mallet and season it with rosemary.
6. Heat the remaining ¼ cup of the dressing in a skillet.
7. Add meat into it to cook for 4 minutes per side.
8. Serve the cooked pork with the prepared rice.

NUTRITION FACTS

Serving 4		
Amount per serving		
Calories		466
		% Daily Value*
Total Fat	12.1g	16%
Saturated Fat	3.4g	17%
Cholesterol	71mg	24%
Sodium	1101mg	48%
Total Carbohydrate	51.6g	19%
Dietary Fiber	3.4g	12%
Total Sugars	8.2g	
Protein	35g	
Vitamin D	0mcg	0%
Calcium	178mg	14%
Iron	5mg	30%
Potassium	870mg	19%

BLUE CHEESE-TOPPED PORK CHOPS

Broiled pork chops are easy to make and easy to serve recipe which is seasoned with cayenne pepper and served with blue cheese, tomato, rosemary, and Italian dressing. it can be best served with the fresh salad.

| **Preparation time:** 5 minutes | **Cooking time:** 20 minutes | **Allergens:** Dairy |

INGREDIENTS

- 2 tablespoons bottled fat-free Italian salad dressing
- Dash cayenne pepper
- 4 5 to 6-ounce bone-in pork loin chops
- ¼ cup crumbled reduced-fat blue cheese (1 ounce)
- 1 tablespoon snipped fresh rosemary

NUTRITION FACTS

Serving 4		
Amount per serving		
Calories		506
		% Daily Value*
Total Fat	21.6g	28%
Saturated Fat	3.7g	18%
Cholesterol	193mg	64%
Sodium	246mg	11%
Total Carbohydrate	3.3g	1%
Dietary Fiber	0.9g	3%
Total Sugars	1.6g	
Protein	70.8g	
Vitamin D	0mcg	0%
Calcium	56mg	4%
Iron	1mg	8%
Potassium	139mg	3%

INSTRUCTIONS

1. Let your oven preheat it at broiler settings.
2. Mix the salad dressing with cayenne pepper.
3. Brush this dressing mixture on both sides of the pork chops liberally.
4. Place the pork chops on the broiler tray, lined with a foil sheet.
5. Broil the pork chops in the broiler 10 minutes about 4 inches below the heat source.
6. Flip the chops after 5 minutes of broiling.
7. Serve the chops with cheese, and rosemary.
8. Enjoy.

ROASTED PEPPER MEAT LOAF

Enjoy a new, rather delicious twist with your meatloaf with this roasted pepper recipe. The saucy combination of minced meat is baked with crumbs to gets a crunchy bite every time. Serve warm with fresh bread to get the best taste

Preparation time: 10 minutes	**Cooking time:** 1hr 30 minutes	**Allergens:** wheat

INGREDIENTS

- 1 (12-ounce) jar roasted red peppers, drained
- 1½ cups whole-wheat bread crumbs
- 2 eggs, lightly beaten
- 1/3 cup purchased tomato sauce
- ½ cup snipped fresh basil
- ¼ cup snipped fresh flat-leaf parsley
- ½ teaspoon salt
- ¼ teaspoon ground black pepper
- 2 pounds 95 percent-lean ground beef
- Snipped fresh flat-leaf parsley

NUTRITION FACTS

Serving 6		
Amount per serving		
Calories		346
		% Daily Value*
Total Fat	18.2g	23%
Saturated Fat	5.6g	28%
Cholesterol	157mg	52%
Sodium	334mg	15%
Total Carbohydrate	20.8g	18%
Dietary Fiber	4.3g	15%
Total Sugars	7.9g	
Protein	27.9g	
Vitamin D	8mcg	39%
Calcium	34mg	3%
Iron	6mg	31%
Potassium	843mg	18%

INSTRUCTIONS

1. Let your oven preheat at 350° F (177° C).
2. Finely chop the roasted peppers and add them to a bowl.
3. Toss in crumbs, basil, salt, egg product, black pepper, parsley, and tomato sauce.
4. Once well combined add ground beef and mix again to combine.
5. Use a loaf pan and grease it with cooking spray.
6. Spread an even layer of beef in the loaf pan.
7. Bake the beef loaf for 1 hour and 20 minutes in the preheated oven.
8. Once done, remove the loaf from its pan after cooling it for 10 minutes.
9. Slice and serve to enjoy with bread.

HERBED BEEF SKEWERS

There is nothing more delicious than having to enjoy juicy beef skewers, and when it is seasoned with a combination of dry herbs, lemon juice, and basic spices, such skewers get irresistible. they are best to add to your BBQ menu.

| **Preparation time:** 15 minutes | **Cooking time:** 20 minutes | **Allergens:** |

INGREDIENTS
- 2 lbs. beef sirloin, cut into cubes
- 3 garlic cloves, minced
- 1 tablespoon fresh lemon zest
- 1 tablespoon fresh parsley, minced
- 2 teaspoon fresh thyme, minced
- 2 teaspoon fresh rosemary, minced
- 2 teaspoon dried oregano
- 4 tablespoons olive oil
- 2 tablespoons fresh lemon juice
- Sea salt and freshly ground black pepper
- Wood or metal skewers

INSTRUCTIONS
1. Use all the ingredients except beef to prepare the marinade.
2. Mix them well together first in a bowl then adjust seasoning as per taste.
3. Place the beef in this marinade and flip it to coat well from all the sides.
4. Marinate the beef in the refrigerator for 20 minutes or overnight.
5. About 30 minutes before the serving, prepare the grill and preheat it.
6. Meanwhile, remove the beef from its marinade and start threading it on the skewers.
7. Grill each skewer for 4 minutes per side on a greased grilling grate.
8. Check if the meat is done, then transfer the grilled beef to the serving plate.
9. Serve immediately with your favorite sauce.

NUTRITION FACTS

Serving 6		
Amount per serving		
Calories		531
		% Daily Value*
Total Fat	21.4g	27%
Saturated Fat	10.4g	52%
Cholesterol	24mg	8%
Sodium	163mg	7%
Total Carbohydrate	57.9g	21%
Dietary Fiber	3.7g	13%
Total Sugars	4.6g	
Protein	30.1g	
Vitamin D	0mcg	0%
Calcium	277mg	21%
Iron	3mg	16%
Potassium	370mg	8%

VEGETABLES LAMB SHANKS

BEEF, PORK AND LAMB RECIPES

To add more colors to your Mediterranean platter, try this lamb shanks recipe which is a complete package of proteins and minerals and vitamins. The seasoned baked shanks are cooked with vegetables.

Preparation Time: 05 Minutes	**Cooking Time:** v2hrs. 45 minutes	**Allergens:**

INGREDIENTS

For Spice Mix
- 2 1/4 teaspoon garlic powder
- 1 teaspoon sweet Spanish paprika
- 1 teaspoon salt
- 1 teaspoon freshly ground black pepper
- 3/4 teaspoon nutmeg, ground

For Lamb
- 6 Lamb Shanks
- 2 tablespoons olive oil
- 1 medium yellow onion, roughly chopped
- 2 celery ribs, chopped
- 3 large carrots, peeled and diced
- 1 lb. baby potatoes, scrubbed
- 2 cups dry red wine
- 3 cups low-sodium beef broth
- 1 (28-oz) can peeled tomatoes
- 2 cinnamon sticks
- 4 sprigs fresh thyme
- 2 sprigs fresh rosemary

INSTRUCTIONS

1. Let your oven preheat at 350° F (177° C)
2. Take a suitable bowl and mix all the spices in it.
3. Dry out the shanks by patting it with a paper towel.
4. Rub the mixture of spice over the lamb liberally.
5. Put a Dutch oven on medium-high heat and pour 2 tbsp oil in it.
6. Add the shanks to the oil to sear it for 5 to 8 minutes per side.
7. Remove the excess fat from the Dutch oven and add onions, carrots, celery, and potatoes.
8. Sauté all the vegetables for 7 mins approximately then stir in red wine.
9. First, deglaze the pot then add tomatoes, cinnamon, rosemary, broth, and thyme.
10. Use more salt and pepper to adjust the seasoning as per taste.
11. After 10 minutes of cooking turn off the heat and cover the Dutch oven.
12. Place this covered Dutch oven in the preheated oven.
13. Let it stay for 2.5 hours until meat is al dente.

NUTRITION FACTS

Servings: 6		
Amount per serving		
Calories		369
		% Daily Value*
Total Fat	18.9g	24%
Saturated Fat	5g	25%
Cholesterol	135mg	45%
Sodium	102mg	4%
Total Carbohydrate	1.7g	1%
Dietary Fiber	0.6g	2%
Total Sugars	0.2g	
Protein	46.2g	
Vitamin D	0mcg	0%
Calcium	26mg	2%
Iron	29mg	163%
Potassium	643mg	14%

GRILLED LONDON BROIL

BEEF, PORK AND LAMB RECIPES

Warm up your grills and make a juicy steak with at home with this grilled London broil recipe. A steak is flavored with a juicy mixture of garlic, cider, and basic spices. These ingredients together with the strong Smokey taste, make this steak a must to have for every table.

Preparation time: 15 minutes	**Cooking time:** 15 minutes	**Allergens:**

INGREDIENTS

- 1/4 cup red wine vinegar
- 1 tablespoon apple cider vinegar
- 2 cloves garlic, minced
- 1 teaspoon dried oregano
- 1/2 teaspoon freshly ground black pepper
- 1/4 cup olive oil
- 2 pounds steak, London Broil

NUTRITION FACTS

Serving 6		
Amount per serving		
Calories		541
		% Daily Value*
Total Fat	31.3g	40%
Saturated Fat	9.9g	50%
Cholesterol	134mg	45%
Sodium	173mg	8%
Total Carbohydrate	0.7g	0%
Dietary Fiber	0.2g	1%
Total Sugars	0.1g	
Protein	60.5g	
Vitamin D	0mcg	0%
Calcium	32mg	2%
Iron	7mg	37%
Potassium	686mg	15%

INSTRUCTIONS

1. Add oil, pepper, garlic, vinegar, and oregano to a Ziplock bag.
2. Zip this bag to seal and shake it well to mix the marinade well.
3. Place the steak in this marinade and seal the bag again.
4. Refrigerate it steak for 2 hours to marinate.
5. About 30 minutes before, prepare the grill and preheat.
6. Remove the steak from its marinade and place it on the greased grill.
7. Cook it for 7 minutes per side in the grill.
8. Once done, allow the steak to cool on a wire rack for 5 minutes.
9. Serve warm with your favorite sauce.

THE COMPLETE MEDITERRANEAN COOKBOOK 2019 EDITION

LAMB PASTA & CHEESE

If you are looking for a cheese rich delight, then this lamb pasta bake is the perfect option for you. The cheese mixed pasta is layered on top of the sautéed lamb mixture. it is baked to a nice melt.

Preparation Time: 10 Minutes	**Cooking Time:** 1hr. 40 minutes	**Allergens:** wheat, Dairy

INGREDIENTS
- 1 tablespoon olive oil
- 1 large onion, chopped
- 2 garlic cloves, crushed
- 1 lb. Lean lamb mince
- 1 teaspoon ground cinnamon
- 1 beef or lamb stock cube
- 2 x 14 oz. Cans chopped tomatoes
- 1 tablespoon dried oregano
- 14 oz. Penne pasta
- 1 1/4 cup ricotta
- 1/4 cup parmesan, grated
- ¼ cup milk
- garlic bread, to serve (optional)

INSTRUCTIONS

1. Take a medium sized skillet and heat oil in it.
2. Add onion, sauté for 10 minutes then stir in garlic.
3. After cooking for a minute add lamb mince.
4. Stir cook until it turns brown in color.
5. Add oregano, cinnamon, tomatoes, and stock cubes.
6. Cover this saucy mixture and cook for 10 minutes with occasional stirring.
7. Meanwhile, boil water to cook macaroni's until they are al dente.
8. Drain and rinse the macaroni under cold water.
9. Let your oven preheat at 375o f (191 o c).
10. Take a large bowl and mix parmesan, milk, seasoning, and ricotta in it.
11. Add the drained macaroni and mix it with the cheese mixture.
12. Grease a suitable baking dish with cooking spray and spread lamb sauce in it.
13. Top it with penne and cheese mixture evenly.
14. Put the dish in the preheated oven to bake for 30 minutes.
15. Serve warm.

NUTRITION FACTS

Servings: **6**	
Amount per serving	
Calories	544
	% Daily Value*
Total Fat 21.4g	27%
Saturated Fat 10.4g	52%
Cholesterol 24mg	8%
Sodium 163mg	7%
Total Carbohydrate 57.9g	21%
Dietary Fiber 3.7g	13%
Total Sugars 4.6g	
Protein 30.1g	
Vitamin D 0mcg	0%
Calcium 277mg	21%
Iron 3mg	16%
Potassium 370mg	8%

SPINACH BEEF PINWHEELS

Beef pinwheel is a charm for every dinner table. The pounded and seasoned beef is stuffed with a layer of spinach and cheese. Such a steak is rolled and sliced; then it is baked well to give a pinwheel-shaped beef patty.

Preparation Time: 10 Minutes	**Cooking Time:** 1hr. 45 minutes	**Allergens:** Dairy

INGREDIENTS

- 1 (2 lbs.) beef Flank Steak
- 1/3 cup lemon juice
- 2 tablespoons vegetable oil
- 2 tablespoons dried oregano leaves
- 1/3 cup olive tapenade
- 1 cup frozen spinach, chopped
- 1/4 cup crumbled low-fat feta cheese
- 4 cups grape or cherry tomatoes
- 1/2 teaspoon salt

INSTRUCTIONS

1. First, place the steak in between two plastic sheets and pound it with a mallet.
2. Take a suitable bowl and toss in all the marinade ingredients.
3. Place the pounded meat in a shallow dish and pour over the marinade.
4. Coat the meat well with the marinade.
5. Cover this dish and refrigerate it for 4 hours to marinate.
6. Let your oven preheat at 425° F (218° C).
7. Take a suitable baking dish and line it with parchment paper.
8. Remove the meat from the marinade and place it on a cutting surface.
9. Add the layer of tapenade, spinach, and feta over the meat steak.
10. Start rolling this steak one side of the rectangle and make a roll.
11. Tie it using butcher thread at different places to keep the meat rolled.
12. Slice this roll cross-sectionally into 6 pinwheels.
13. Place these slices with their cut side down in the baking dish.
14. Pour the left-over marinade over the pinwheels.
15. Place them in the preheated oven for 35 minutes approximately.
16. Serve immediately.

NUTRITION FACTS

Servings: 4		
Amount per serving		
Calories		569
		% Daily Value*
Total Fat	22.4g	29%
Saturated Fat	7.5g	37%
Cholesterol	205mg	68%
Sodium	538mg	23%
Total Carbohydrate	18.2g	7%
Dietary Fiber	2g	7%
Total Sugars	15.5g	
Protein	71.3g	
Vitamin D	0mcg	0%
Calcium	75mg	6%
Iron	44mg	245%
Potassium	1194mg	25%

ROMESCO GLAZED BEEF STEAK

If you love to enjoy Romesco every now and then, this beef steak recipe will catch you by its taste and aroma. The grilled steak is served with Romesco sauce on top along with hummus, pine nuts, olive, and feta cheese.

Preparation Time: 10 Minutes	**Cooking Time:** 15 minutes	**Allergens:** Dairy

INGREDIENTS

- 1-pound beef sirloin steaks, boneless, cut 1 inch thick
- 1/4 cup chopped fresh oregano leaves
- 1 tablespoon grated lemon peel
- 1 tablespoon plus 1 teaspoon minced garlic
- 1 teaspoon pepper
- 1 medium cucumber, thinly sliced
- 3 tablespoons fresh lemon juice
- 1/4 teaspoon pepper
- 2 tablespoons Romesco Sauce
- 1 cup hummus

INSTRUCTIONS

1. Take a shallow dish and place the beef steaks in this dish.
2. Rub the dry spices on both sides of the steaks liberally.
3. Prepare the grill and preheat it on medium heat.
4. Place the seasoned steak on the greased grilling grates of the grill.
5. Grill the steak for 14 minutes while flipping after every 5 minutes.
6. Meanwhile, toss cucumber with pepper and lemon juice in a suitable bowl.
7. Add the ingredients for the Romesco in a food processor.
8. Place the grilled steak in the serving plate and slice it.
9. Drizzle salt, pepper and Romesco sauce over it.
10. Add hummus, cucumber strips, olives, feta cheese and pine nuts to the same plate.
11. Serve immediately.

NUTRITION FACTS

Servings: 4		
Amount per serving		
Calories		355
		% Daily Value*
Total Fat	14.4g	18%
Saturated Fat	3.9g	19%
Cholesterol	101mg	34%
Sodium	330mg	14%
Total Carbohydrate	16.5g	6%
Dietary Fiber	6.6g	23%
Total Sugars	2g	
Protein	40.8g	
Vitamin D	0mcg	0%
Calcium	118mg	9%
Iron	25mg	141%
Potassium	816mg	17%

MINT BEEF SKEWERS

These skewers are made out of minced beef. The meat is mixed with mint, allspice, and other spices and then it is grilled on the skewers in shape of kebab. These skewers taste scrumptious when served with a pesto sauce or savory mint sauce.

Preparation time: 15 minutes	**Cooking time:** 15 minutes	**Allergens:**

INGREDIENTS

- 1-pound Ground Beef (93% lean or leaner)
- 1/2 cup minced onions
- 1 tablespoon olive oil
- 1/2 teaspoon salt
- 1/2 teaspoon ground coriander
- 1/2 teaspoon ground cumin
- 1/4 teaspoon ground cinnamon
- 1/4 teaspoon allspice
- 1/4 teaspoon dried mint leaves

INSTRUCTIONS

1. Combine beef with salt, allspice, coriander, oil, onion, mint, cinnamon, and cumin in a bowl.
2. Take each skewer and make an elongated kebab over it using this beef mixture.
3. Place all the kebab skewers in a shallow tray and refrigerate them for 10 minutes.
4. Meanwhile, prepare the grill on medium heat.
5. Grease the grilling grates and grill the kebabs for 5 minutes per side or more.
6. Serve immediately.

NUTRITION FACTS

Serving 2	
Amount per serving	
Calories	496
	% Daily Value*
Total Fat 21.3g	27%
Saturated Fat 6.4g	32%
Cholesterol 203mg	68%
Sodium 733mg	32%
Total Carbohydrate 3.3g	1%
Dietary Fiber 0.9g	3%
Total Sugars 1.2g	
Protein 69.2g	
Vitamin D 0mcg	0%
Calcium 20mg	2%
Iron 43mg	240%
Potassium 970mg	21%

BAKED LAMB TRAY

The lamb tray is a perfect weekend night dinner meal to serve all your needs. It is a blend of both the good taste and a great combination of nutrients. The minced lamb patties are baked over a layer of juicy vegetables.

Preparation time: 15 minutes	**Cooking time:** 40 minutes	**Allergens:** wheat, Dairy

INGREDIENTS
- 1/4 cup fresh white breadcrumbs
- 1 1/4 cup lamb mince
- 1 egg, beaten
- 2 onions, halved
- large handful mint, chopped
- 2 large potatoes, cut into wedges
- 2 zucchinis, cut into batons
- 12 cherry tomatoes
- 2 tablespoons olive oil
- 1/4 cup feta cheese, crumbled

INSTRUCTIONS
1. Let your oven preheat at 350° F (177° C).
2. Mix the lamb mince with crumbs, seasoning, and egg in a glass bowl.
3. Add half of the grated onion and chopped mint.
4. After mixing it all well make 8 small patties out of it.
5. Place the patties in a roasting pan and surround them with onion wedges, potatoes, tomatoes, and zucchinis.
6. Top the patties with oil and seasoning then bake them for 40 mins.
7. Once done, garnish these patties with remaining mint and feta cheese.
8. Serve immediately.

NUTRITION FACTS

Serving 4		
Amount per serving		
Calories		599
		% Daily Value*
Total Fat	28.3g	36%
Saturated Fat	9.9g	50%
Cholesterol	132mg	44%
Sodium	279mg	12%
Total Carbohydrate	16.7g	21%
Dietary Fiber	11.4g	41%
Total Sugars	1.2g	
Protein	32.8g	
Vitamin D	4mcg	19%
Calcium	164mg	13%
Iron	5mg	25%
Potassium	2284mg	49%

SOUP RECIPES

Cannellini Beans Soup

Red Barley Soup

Tuscan Bean Soup

Ditalini Minestrone

Greek Meatball Soup

Zucchini Soup

Grilled Vegetable soup

Napoletana Hoki soup

White Celeriac soup

Passata Cream Soup

Tortellini soup

THE COMPLETE MEDITERRANEAN COOKBOOK 2019 EDITION

CANNELLINI BEANS SOUP

A bowl of soup cooked with chunky vegetables, and beans are what can make your day. The warming recipe is cooked with loads of cooking liquid, simply seasoning, cannellini beans, and cheese toppings.

Preparation Time: 10 Minutes	**Cooking Time:** 1 hr. 15 minutes	**Allergens:** Dairy

INGREDIENTS

- 8 oz. dried Cannellini beans
- 4 tablespoons olive oil
- 1 onion, finely chopped
- 3 garlic cloves, finely chopped
- 1 celery stalk, chopped
- 3 sprigs fresh thyme
- 2 bay leaves
- ¼-½ teaspoon pepper
- 5 cups of water
- 1 teaspoon. salt
- ½ Lemon (juice)
- 3 tablespoons olive oil
- 2 shallots, sliced into rings
- Parmesan cheese shaved
- Extra virgin olive oil for drizzling

INSTRUCTIONS

1. Fill a large bowl with water up to 2/3 full and soak beans in it overnight.
2. Drain the soaked beans the next day and keep them aside.
3. Let the oil heat in a cooking pan over medium heat.
4. Stir in onion and sauté until it turns golden.
5. Add garlic and stir cook for 1 minute.
6. Stir in black pepper, beans, thyme, bay leaf, and celery.
7. Add water to the soup base and cook it to a boil.
8. Later cook the mixture for 1 hour on a simmer until the beans are al dente.
9. Discard the bay leaves and adjust seasoning with lemon juice and salt.
10. Meanwhile, sauté shallots for 5 minutes in a greased heated pan.
11. Garnish the cooked beans soup with parmesan, olive oil, and sauté onion.
12. Serve instantly.

NUTRITION FACTS

Servings: 4	
Amount per serving	
Calories	327
	% Daily Value*
Total Fat 14.6g	19%
Saturated Fat 2.1g	11%
Cholesterol 0mg	0%
Sodium 28mg	1%
Total Carbohydrate 38.3g	14%
Dietary Fiber 15.2g	54%
Total Sugars 2.5g	
Protein 13.9g	
Vitamin D 0mcg	0%
Calcium 119mg	9%
Iron 6mg	33%
Potassium 870mg	19%

RED BARLEY SOUP

Barley is a source of essential nutrients, fibers, and vitamins, being the basic ingredient of this soup, it makes it highly nutritious for people of all age. And that is not it; the barley is paired with red lentils, mixed vegetables, and tomato sauce.

Preparation Time: 10 Minutes	**Cooking Time:** 60 minutes	**Allergens:** Dairy

INGREDIENTS

- ½ lb. dried, small, red lentils
- ½ cup barley
- ½ cup olive oil
- 2 small onions, diced
- 2 medium carrots, diced
- 1 stalk celery
- 6 cloves garlic
- 2 bay leaves
- 1½ cups tomato sauce
- 7 cups of water
- 1-2 teaspoon. smoked paprika
- 1 tablespoon dried Greek oregano
- 1 teaspoon salt
- Black pepper to taste
- 3 tablespoons red wine or Balsamic vinegar
- Cheese to serve
- Brown bread cubes, to serve

INSTRUCTIONS

1. Wash the lentils under cold water and rinse properly.
2. Add those lentils to a suitably sized cooking pot
3. Pour just enough water to cover the lentils.
4. Cook it first to a boil then simmer for 5 mins.
5. Stir in barley, along with all the other ingredients.
6. After adding 6 cups of water to the pot, cover it to cook for 40 minutes.
7. Check the consistency of the soup and cook more for 5-10 minutes until it thickens.
8. Discard the bay leaves and garnish with cheese.
9. Serve warm with bread.

NUTRITION FACTS

Servings: 4	
Amount per serving Calories	470
	% Daily Value*
Total Fat 26.9g	34%
Saturated Fat 3.8g	19%
Cholesterol 0mg	0%
Sodium 2391mg	104%
Total Carbohydrate 51.5g	19%
Dietary Fiber 13.2g	47%
Total Sugars 18g	
Protein 11.8g	
Vitamin D 0mcg	0%
Calcium 119mg	9%
Iron 6mg	33%
Potassium 1552mg	33%

TUSCAN BEAN SOUP

What more you could ask for when your favorite pasta, beans, and all the vegetables are brought together in a single bowl of soup. this is why Tuscan bean soup, is served as a complete meal in itself.

Preparation Time: 10 Minutes   **Cooking Time:** 20 minutes   **Allergens:** wheat, Dairy

INGREDIENTS

- 4 oz. Pancetta, cut in small cubes
- 3 tablespoons olive oil
- 1 onion, finely chopped
- 1 carrot, peeled and chopped finely
- 1 celery stalk, chopped finely
- 3 garlic cloves, minced
- 1 sprig fresh rosemary, minced
- 1 pepperoncino, minced, optional
- 16 oz. Canned italian plum tomatoes, pureed
- 1 lb. Cranberry cooked beans
- 3-4 cups chicken stock, hot
- 1 teaspoon salt
- pepper, to taste
- ½ lb. Ditalini pasta (or other small sized pasta)
- 1 tablespoons butter
- 5 tablespoons parmigiano reggiano cheese, grated

INSTRUCTIONS

1. Place a cooking pan on medium heat with cooking oil in it.
2. Stir in pancetta cubes and sauté until golden brown from all the sides.
3. Add onion, celery, and carrot, sauté for 2 minutes.
4. Stir in garlic, pepperoncino and rosemary, cook until veggies are soft.
5. Add the tomatoes with their juices – Cook for 5 minutes.
6. Stir in drained beans, cook for another 10 minutes.
7. Add seasonings and stock. to cook pasta, boil this soup.
8. Stir in pasta and cook the soup until it is al dente.
9. Gently squash the beans in the soup then add cheese and butter.
10. Adjust seasoning then serve warm.

NUTRITION FACTS

Servings: 6	
Amount per serving	
Calories	486
	% Daily Value*
Total Fat 20.9g	27%
Saturated Fat 6.7g	33%
Cholesterol 33mg	11%
Sodium 1322mg	57%
Total Carbohydrate 54.5g	20%
Dietary Fiber 10.5g	38%
Total Sugars 6g	
Protein 23.2g	
Vitamin D 1mcg	7%
Calcium 155mg	12%
Iron 4mg	20%
Potassium 636mg	14%

DITALINI MINESTRONE

You cannot enjoy a Mediterranean diet without adding a bowl of minestrone soup to your routine menu. This soup is made with a combination of vegetables including carrots, celery, and cabbage, which are cooked in hot stock along with beans and pasta.

Preparation Time: 10 Minutes	**Cooking Time:** 20 minutes	**Allergens:** gluten, Dairy

INGREDIENTS
- ¼ cup olive oil
- 1 onion, chopped
- 2 carrots, chopped
- 2 celery stalks, chopped
- 3 garlic cloves, minced
- 1 teaspoon salt
- ¼ teaspoon pepper
- 2 cups of water
- 4 cups chicken stock
- ½ cup tomato sauce
- 3 sprigs fresh thyme
- 1 bay leaf
- 2 cups spinach or swiss chard, chopped
- 1 cup napa cabbage, chopped
- 1 can cannellini beans
- 2/3 cup ditalini pasta
- 1 pinch red pepper flakes
- paresan cheese ribbons for garnish
- extra virgin olive oil to drizzle

INSTRUCTIONS

1. Take A Cooking Pot And Heat Olive Oil In It.
2. Stir In Celery, Onion, And Carrots, Sauté Until They Are Soft.
3. Add Salt, Pepper, And Garlic, Stir Cook For 1 Min.
4. Pour In The Stock, Water, Tomato Sauce And Add Thyme And Bay Leaf.
5. Boil The Soup Then Add Red Pepper Flakes, Spinach, And Cabbage.
6. Cook The Soup Until The Veggies Turn Soft.
7. Add In The Pasta And Cook Until It Is Al Dente.
8. Garnish It With Lemon Juice, Parmesan Cheese, And Olive Oil.
9. Serve Immediately.

NUTRITION FACTS

Servings: 4		
Amount per serving		
Calories		346
		% Daily Value*
Total Fat	13.9g	18%
Saturated Fat	2g	10%
Cholesterol	0mg	0%
Sodium	1573mg	68%
Total Carbohydrate	44.6g	16%
Dietary Fiber	14.3g	51%
Total Sugars	6.5g	
Protein	14.6g	
Vitamin D	0mcg	0%
Calcium	146mg	11%
Iron	5mg	29%
Potassium	1064mg	23%

GREEK MEATBALL SOUP

The Greek meatball soup is a special delicacy of the Mediterranean states, and it is mostly served and loved because of the unique lemon-egg mixture which is added to the soup once it is cooked.

Preparation Time: 10 Minutes   **Cooking Time:** 30 minutes   **Allergens:** wheat, egg

INGREDIENTS

For the Meatballs
- 1 lb. lean ground beef
- ½ cup medium grain rice
- 1 small onion grated
- ½ fresh parsley, minced
- 3 tablespoons fresh dill, minced
- 1½ teaspoon. salt
- ½ teaspoon. pepper
- 2 tablespoons olive oil
- 2 tablespoons water
- ½ cup of whole wheat flour

For the egg-lemon broth
- 1 whole egg and two egg yolks
- 3-4 tablespoons lemon juice (one medium lemon)
- 2 teaspoon cornstarch

INSTRUCTIONS

1. Stir the meat with rice, dill, salt, parsley, water, olive oil, pepper and onion in a suitable bowl.
2. Cover this meat mixture and place it in the refrigerator for 15 minutes.
3. Use this mixture to make 30 meatballs of golf balls size.
4. Prepare the soup by boiling 8 cups water in a large soup pot.
5. Add ½ teaspoon salt and 3 tablespoons olive oil.
6. Place the meatballs in this soup and cover it partially.
7. Cook the soup for 30 mins approximately, on a simmer.
8. Beat egg with egg yolks in a suitable bowl until frothy.
9. Mix cornstarch with lemon juice.
10. Gradually pour the cornstarch slurry into the soup while stirring the soup.
11. Once the soup turns creamy, stir in the egg mixture with stirring.
12. Garnish with olive oil and parsley.
13. Enjoy.

NUTRITION FACTS

Servings: 4		
Amount per serving		
Calories		480
		% Daily Value*
Total Fat	17.9g	23%
Saturated Fat	4.9g	24%
Cholesterol	224mg	75%
Sodium	131mg	6%
Total Carbohydrate	35.1g	13%
Dietary Fiber	1.5g	5%
Total Sugars	1.3g	
Protein	42.6g	
Vitamin D	12mcg	58%
Calcium	74mg	6%
Iron	25mg	138%
Potassium	661mg	14%

ZUCCHINI SOUP

This mushroom zucchini soup is famous for its ultimate richness. From chopped mushrooms to the sliced zucchinis, carrots, potatoes, celery, and chickpeas, everything is a part of this soup.

Preparation Time: 10 Minutes   **Cooking Time:** 20 minutes   **Allergens:** Pine Nuts

INGREDIENTS

- Olive oil
- 8 oz. sliced baby Bella mushrooms
- 2 medium-size zucchinis, tops removed, sliced into rounds or half-moons
- 1 bunch flat leaf parsley, chopped
- 1 medium-size yellow or red onion, chopped
- 2 garlic cloves, chopped
- 2 celery ribs, chopped
- 2 carrots, peeled, chopped
- 2 golden potatoes, peeled, diced
- 1 teaspoon ground coriander
- 1/2 teaspoon turmeric powder
- 1/2 teaspoon sweet paprika
- 1/2 teaspoon thyme
- Salt and pepper
- 1 32-oz can whole peeled tomatoes
- 2 bay leaves
- 6 cups turkey bone broth
- 1 15-oz can chickpeas, rinsed and drained
- Zest of 1 lime
- Juice of 1 lime
- 1/3 cup toasted pine nuts, optional

INSTRUCTIONS

1. Preheat 1 tablespoon olive oil in an iron cooking pot on medium heat.
2. Stir in mushrooms and sauté them for 4 minutes.
3. Transfer the mushrooms to a flat plate and keep them aside.
4. Toss the sliced zucchini into the pot and sauté for 5 mins approximately.
5. Again, transfer the sautéed zucchini to a plate.
6. Heat more oil in that same pan and add celery, potatoes, garlic, and onion.
7. Stir cook these veggies for 7 minutes.
8. Season the mixture with pepper, salt, and other spices.
9. Stir in bay leaves, tomatoes, and broth — Cook this soup to a boil.
10. Cover the soup with a lid and now cook it on a simmer for 5 mins approximately.
11. Uncover the soup then add chickpeas, sautéed mushrooms, and zucchini.
12. Let the soup cook for 5 mins more, then garnish with pine nuts.
13. Serve warm.

NUTRITION FACTS

Servings: 6		
Amount per serving		
Calories		470
		% Daily Value*
Total Fat	10.2g	13%
Saturated Fat	0.9g	5%
Cholesterol	0mg	0%
Sodium	1040mg	45%
Total Carbohydrate	78.9g	29%
Dietary Fiber	18.9g	68%
Total Sugars	16.7g	
Protein	22.6g	
Vitamin D	0mcg	0%
Calcium	131mg	10%
Iron	7mg	41%
Potassium	1974mg	42%

GRILLED VEGETABLE SOUP

This soup is a perfect vegetarian treat for every occasion. No extra spices or seasonings, this soup is all vegetables, stock, tomato, and basil. It is served warm with ricotta and rye bread for best taste.

Preparation time: 15 minutes	**Cooking time:** 25 minutes	**Allergens:**

INGREDIENTS

- 14oz. frozen grilled vegetable mix: peppers, aubergine, onion, zucchinis
- 2 tablespoons chopped garlic
- handful basil leaves
- 14 oz. can chop tomato
- 1 reduced-salt vegetable stock cube

NUTRITION FACTS

Serving 2		
Amount per serving		
Calories		171
		% Daily Value*
Total Fat	2.9g	4%
Saturated Fat	1.7g	8%
Cholesterol	10mg	3%
Sodium	406mg	18%
Total Carbohydrate	27.3g	10%
Dietary Fiber	7.7g	28%
Total Sugars	5.8g	
Protein	9.3g	
Vitamin D	0mcg	0%
Calcium	144mg	11%
Iron	2mg	10%
Potassium	371mg	8%

INSTRUCTIONS

1. Sauté garlic in a greased and heat pan for 30 seconds.
2. Stir in half of the vegetables and sauté them for 5 minutes.
3. Add 2 cups of water, tomatoes, and stock cubes.
4. Stir cook until this mixture is well combined and smooth.
5. Use a hand blender to puree this mixture.
6. Add the remaining half of the vegetables and cook for 20 mins.
7. Enjoy.

NAPOLETANA HOKI SOUP

The pasta sauce of this soup gives its unique taste among all the vegetable soups. It is made out of fish stock and Hoki fillets, that is why the soup is a direct source of seafood and several vitamins and minerals.

Preparation time: 15 minutes	**Cooking time:** 20 minutes	**Allergens:**

INGREDIENTS

- 1 lb. Napoletana (tomato and basil) pasta sauce
- 2 cups fish stock
- 2 zucchinis, finely sliced
- 1 bulb fennel, finely sliced
- 1 lb. hoki fillet, defrosted
- handful basil leaves, torn
- 1 teaspoon chipotle chili in adobo sauce or chili paste, to serve
- 5 tablespoons half-fat crème Fraiche, to serve

INSTRUCTIONS

1. Take a large cooking pan and mix pasta sauce with stock in it.
2. After boiling this soup, let it simmer for 3 minutes.
3. Stir in zucchinis and fennel, then cook for 2 mins.
4. Add the hoki fillets to the soup after slicing them down into pieces.
5. Let it cook for 3 minutes on low heat.
6. Adjust seasoning and add basil to the soup.
7. Mix crème Fraiche with chili paste and season in a small bowl.
8. Garnish the soup with this seasoned crème Fraiche.
9. Enjoy.

NUTRITION FACTS

Serving 4		
Amount per serving		
Calories		459
		% Daily Value*
Total Fat	21.8g	28%
Saturated Fat	3.7g	18%
Cholesterol	17mg	6%
Sodium	1312mg	57%
Total Carbohydrate	44.5g	16%
Dietary Fiber	5.7g	20%
Total Sugars	7.5g	
Protein	18.6g	
Vitamin D	0mcg	0%
Calcium	131mg	10%
Iron	2mg	12%
Potassium	667mg	14%

WHITE CELERIAC SOUP

It is a nutty and creamy soup which is made out of potato and celeriac base. The soup is flavored with the soy cream, which gives it a cloudy appearance and richness to the taste. it is served warm with hazelnuts and truffle oil.

Preparation time: 10 minutes	**Cooking time:** 40 minutes	**Allergens:** soy, hazelnuts

INGREDIENTS

- 1 tablespoon olive oil
- small bunch thyme
- 2 bay leave
- 1 onion, chopped
- 1 garlic clove, chopped
- 1 celeriac, peeled and chopped
- 1 potato (about 7 oz.), chopped
- 4 cups vegetable stock
- 1/2 cup soy cream
- 1/4 cup blanched hazelnuts, toasted and roughly chopped
- 1 tablespoon truffle oil, plus an extra drizzle to serve

INSTRUCTIONS

1. Preheat cooking oil on low heat in an appropriate saucepan.
2. Tie all the thyme sprigs with bay leaves and place this bunch in the pan.
3. Stir in onion along with one pinch salt. Saute for 10 mins until soft.
4. Add garlic, stir cook for a minute then add celeriac and potato.
5. Adjust seasoning with salt and pepper.
6. Pour the stock in and cook it to a boil then simmer the soup for 30 mins.
7. Discard the herbs bunch and add cream to the soup.
8. Puree the soup after turning off the heat using an immersion blender.
9. Adjust seasoning as per taste and add ½ tbsp truffle oil.
10. Garnish with truffle oil and hazelnuts.
11. Serve warm.

NUTRITION FACTS

Serving 4		
Amount per serving		
Calories		157
		% Daily Value*
Total Fat	10.1g	13%
Saturated Fat	1.3g	6%
Cholesterol	0mg	0%
Sodium	93mg	4%
Total Carbohydrate	15.6g	6%
Dietary Fiber	3.2g	12%
Total Sugars	3g	
Protein	2.9g	
Vitamin D	0mcg	0%
Calcium	36mg	3%
Iron	1mg	5%
Potassium	372mg	8%

PASSATA CREAM SOUP

Passata is the special tomato sauce which is used to flavor and enrich this soup. it also contains carrots, celery, and onion, paired with cream and cheese. Serve the hot soup with breadsticks.

| **Preparation time:** 10 minutes | **Cooking time:** 30 minutes | **Allergens:** Soy, Hazelnuts, Dairy |

INGREDIENTS

- 2 tablespoons olive oil
- ½ onion, finely chopped
- 1 small carrot, finely chopped
- 1 celery stick, finely chopped
- 1/2 cup passata
- 4 large ripe tomatoes
- ½ vegetable or chicken stock melt or cube
- 2 tablespoons cream (optional)
- 4oz. soup pasta, cooked
- shaved parmesan, chopped basil or pesto

NUTRITION FACTS

Serving 4		
Amount per serving		
Calories		237
		% Daily Value*
Total Fat	8.4g	11%
Saturated Fat	1.3g	6%
Cholesterol	1mg	0%
Sodium	178mg	8%
Total Carbohydrate	35g	13%
Dietary Fiber	4.6g	16%
Total Sugars	7.7g	
Protein	6.2g	
Vitamin D	0mcg	0%
Calcium	31mg	2%
Iron	1mg	8%
Potassium	520mg	11%

INSTRUCTIONS

1. Let the oil preheat in a saucepan on low heat.
2. Stir in onion, celery, and carrots, sauté for 10 mins until they are soft.
3. Add the passata sauce and tomatoes.
4. While boiling this mixture add water, stock, seasoning, and sugar to it.
5. Cook the soup for 20 mins approximately, on a simmer.
6. Stir in boiled pasta and cream with gentle stirring.
7. Garnish with cheese, basil, and pesto.
8. Enjoy.

TORTELLINI SOUP

Add tortellini to your routine menu, with this pea and beans warming soup. it is all cooked with vegetable stock, carrots, onion and parmesan. Use fresh basil leaves to the garnish this soup.

| **Preparation time:** 10 minutes | **Cooking time:** 20 minutes | **Allergens:** |

INGREDIENTS

- 1 tablespoon olive oil
- 2 carrots, chopped
- 1 large onion, finely chopped
- 4 cups vegetable stock
- 14 oz. can tomato, chopped
- 7 oz. frozen mixed pea and beans
- 1 1/4 cup pack freshly filled tortellini
- a handful of basil leaves (optional)
- grated parmesan, to serve

INSTRUCTIONS

1. Add carrots and onions to a greased and heated pan.
2. Sauté these veggies for 5 minutes then add tomatoes and stock.
3. Cook this mixture for 10 minutes then add peas and beans.
4. After cooking for 5 minutes stir in pasta.
5. Add the pasta to cook in the soup until it is al dente.
6. Add basil and adjust the seasoning.
7. Garnish with bread slice and parmesan.
8. Serve warm.

NUTRITION FACTS

Serving 4		
Amount per serving		
Calories		118
		% Daily Value*
Total Fat	5.5g	7%
Saturated Fat	2.5g	13%
Cholesterol	0mg	0%
Sodium	817mg	36%
Total Carbohydrate	22.8g	8%
Dietary Fiber	3g	11%
Total Sugars	7.7g	
Protein	2.5g	
Vitamin D	0mcg	0%
Calcium	19mg	1%
Iron	1mg	4%
Potassium	257mg	5%

POTATO MUSHROOM SOUP

With this soup recipe, you get to enjoy both the chestnut and porcini mushrooms in a single bowl. The soup is cooked with a bouillon base and bio yogurt. It gets chunkier with the addition of potatoes and carrots.

| **Preparation time:** 10 minutes | **Cooking time:** 30 minutes | **Allergens:** Walnut |

INGREDIENTS

- 1 tablespoon rapeseed oil
- 2 large onions, halved and thinly sliced
- 1 tablespoon dried porcini mushrooms
- 3 teaspoons vegetable bouillon powder
- 4 cups chestnut mushrooms, chopped
- 3 garlic cloves, finely grated
- 4 cups potato, finely diced
- 2 teaspoons fresh thyme
- 4 carrots, finely diced
- 2 tablespoons chopped parsley
- 8 tablespoons bio yogurt
- 2 tablespoons walnut pieces

INSTRUCTIONS

1. Heat the cooking oil in the suitably sized pan.
2. Add onion and sauté it for 10 minutes until golden in color.
3. Meanwhile, mix bouillon in hot water and soak dried mushrooms in it.
4. Now add garlic, thyme, mushrooms, potatoes, and carrots to the onions.
5. Sauté until mushrooms turn golden in color.
6. Pour in the dried mushroom along with their bouillon water into the pan.
7. Cover this soup with a lid and let it cook for 20 mins approximately on a simmer.
8. Garnish with yogurt, walnuts, parsley, and pepper.
9. Serve warm.

NUTRITION FACTS

Serving 4		
Amount per serving		
Calories		264
		% Daily Value*
Total Fat	9.1g	12%
Saturated Fat	1.1g	6%
Cholesterol	2mg	1%
Sodium	256mg	11%
Total Carbohydrate	40.4g	15%
Dietary Fiber	7.5g	27%
Total Sugars	9.2g	
Protein	7.5g	
Vitamin D	0mcg	0%
Calcium	121mg	9%
Iron	3mg	15%
Potassium	886mg	19%

FISH AND SEAFOOD RECIPES

Mixed Seafood Stew

Squid Oyster Medley

Sauce Dipped Mussels

Crusty Grilled Mussels

Seafood Garlic Couscous

Lobster Rice Paella

Fish and Vegetable Parcels

Saffron Fish gratins

THE COMPLETE MEDITERRANEAN COOKBOOK 2019 EDITION

MIXED SEAFOOD STEW

A well-cooked seafood stew can guarantee both health and good taste. it has a variety of seafood, including fish, clam juice, scallops, and the shrimp. The seafood is cooked in the tomato-based sauce.

| **Preparation Time:** 05 Minutes | **Cooking Time:** 15 minutes | **Allergens:** Egg |

INGREDIENTS

- 1 medium onion, finely chopped
- 1 tablespoon olive oil
- 1-1/2 teaspoons minced garlic, divided
- ½ pound plum tomatoes, seeded and diced
- 1 teaspoon grated lemon peel
- ¼ teaspoon red pepper flakes, crushed
- 1/3 cup white wine
- 1 tablespoon tomato paste
- Salt to taste
- 1 oz. red snapper fillets, cut into 1-inch cubes
- 1 lb. shrimp, peeled and deveined
- ½ lb. sea scallops
- 1 cup clam juice
- 1/3 cup minced fresh parsley
- 1/3 cup reduced-fat mayonnaise

INSTRUCTIONS

1. Take a dutch oven in a suitable size and heat it with cooking oil on medium heat.
2. Stir in onion and saute them until it is soft.
3. Add garlic and stir-cook it for a minute.
4. Toss in tomatoes, lemon peel, and pepper flakes.
5. Continue stir cooking for 2 tomatoes.
6. Add the wine, salt, tomato paste, and clam juice.
7. Let this mixture cook to a boil then reduce it to a simmer.
8. Continue cooking for 10 minutes after covering the lid.
9. Gently toss in shrimp, parsley, scallops, and fish.
10. Again, cook for 10 minutes after covering the lid.
11. Garnish with garlic and mayonnaise.
12. Serve warm.

NUTRITION FACTS

Servings: 6	
Amount per serving	
Calories	390
	% Daily Value*
Total Fat 15.3g	20%
Saturated Fat 2.6g	13%
Cholesterol 261mg	87%
Sodium 673mg	29%
Total Carbohydrate 20.1g	7%
Dietary Fiber 1.9g	7%
Total Sugars 7.3g	
Protein 39g	
Vitamin D 0mcg	0%
Calcium 149mg	11%
Iron 2mg	8%
Potassium 717mg	15%

SQUID OYSTER MEDLEY

FISH AND SEAFOOD RECIPES

If you haven't yet any squid recipe, that this seafood medley is the perfect options as it pairs unique ingredients together in a tasty combination. The squid is cooked with oyster, clams, and mussels, imagine the richness of this seafood recipe.

Preparation Time: 05 Minutes	**Cooking Time:** 30 minutes	**Allergens:** milk

INGREDIENTS

- 20 baby squid (tubes and tentacles), cleaned
- 3 cups of milk
- 2 tablespoons extra-virgin olive oil
- 8 cloves garlic, minced
- 2 small onions, chopped
- 2 large carrots, chopped
- 2 tomatoes, chopped
- ½ cup tomato paste
- 1 cup dry white wine
- 3 cups chicken stock
- ½ bunch fresh parsley
- ½ bunch fresh tarragon
- ½ bunch fresh thyme
- 2 bay leaves
- 1 teaspoon black peppercorns
- 1 tablespoon loosely packed saffron threads
- 2 tablespoons extra-virgin olive oil
- 6 cloves garlic, minced
- ½ cup oil-packed sun-dried tomatoes, drained and cut into strips
- 6 baby fennel bulbs, halved
- ½ bunch fresh thyme, chopped
- 10 fresh oysters in shells, well-scrubbed
- 20 littleneck clams
- 20 fresh mussels
- 6 (6 ounce) fillets fresh sea bass
- salt and pepper to taste
- 2 tablespoons extra-virgin olive oil
- 6 sprigs parsley, for garnish

NUTRITION FACTS

Serving 8		
Amount per serving Calories		414
		% Daily Value*
Total Fat	11.3g	15%
Saturated Fat	2.2g	11%
Cholesterol	499mg	166%
Sodium	696mg	30%
Total Carbohydrate	25.6g	9%
Dietary Fiber	2.3g	8%
Total Sugars	10.2g	
Protein	43.2g	
Vitamin D	1mcg	6%
Calcium	266mg	20%
Iron	7mg	38%
Potassium	697mg	

INSTRUCTIONS

1. First, add milk to a large bowl and soak squid in it for 5 hours.
2. Drain the milk and keep the squid aside.
3. Take 2 tablespoons oil in a cooking pan and preheat it.
4. Toss in half of the fennels, carrots, tomatoes, onion, and garlic.
5. Sauté these vegetables for 10 minutes then stir in tomato paste.
6. Cook for another 10 minutes then pour in the wine.
7. After bringing this mixture to a boil then stir in tarragon, saffron, thyme, bay leaves, stock, peppercorns, and parsley.
8. Cook this mixture for 15 minutes on a simmer until it is reduced.
9. Strain this stock and discard all the solids including the vegetables.
10. Preheat another 2 tbsp oil in the same pot.
11. Add garlic, sauté it for 45 secs.
12. Stir in sun-dried tomatoes and remaining fennel.
13. After cooking them for 2 minutes at the vegetables stock and thyme.
14. Boil this soup and add the oysters to the pot.
15. Cook it for a minutes after covering its lid.
16. Uncover the pot then place clams and mussels in the cooking mixture.
17. Cook it for 4 mins approximately then add drained squid.
18. Let it cook for another 1 minute.
19. Meanwhile, sear the fish fillets for 4 minutes per side in a heated greased skillet.
20. Serve the seafood medley with fish fillets on top.
21. Garnish with parsley and enjoy.

SAUCE DIPPED MUSSELS

Rare is the mussel's recipes which are cooked into a such a delicious yet simple meal. it is an all mussel recipe cooked with tomato paste, garlic, and shallots. The dry white wine adds a unique balance to this recipe.

Preparation time: 15 minutes	**Cooking time:** 20 minutes	**Allergens:**

INGREDIENTS

- 2 ripe tomatoes
- 2 tablespoons olive oil
- 1 garlic clove, minced
- 1 shallot, finely diced
- 1 red or green chili, deseeded and Chopped
- 1 small glass dry white wine
- 1 teaspoon tomato paste
- pinch of sugar
- 1 lb. Cleaned mussels
- good handful basil leaves

NUTRITION FACTS

Serving 2	
Amount per serving	
Calories	320
	% Daily Value*
Total Fat 17.8g	23%
Saturated Fat 2.7g	13%
Cholesterol 42mg	14%
Sodium 537mg	23%
Total Carbohydrate 19.4g	7%
Dietary Fiber 2.4g	9%
Total Sugars 6.8g	
Protein 20.3g	
Vitamin D 0mcg	0%
Calcium 67mg	5%
Iron 7mg	38%
Potassium 983mg	21%

INSTRUCTIONS

1. Soak tomatoes in lukewarm water for 3 minutes then drain them.
2. Drain these tomatoes and peel and dice them in four pieces.
3. After removing the seeds, chop the flesh into cubes.
4. Take a deep pan or wok and heat oil in it.
5. Stir in garlic, chili, and shallot, sauté them for 3 minutes.
6. Add seasonings, sugar, wine, and tomatoes.
7. Stir cook this mixture for 2 minutes.
8. Gently place the mussels in the cooking pan and cover them with a lid.
9. After cooking for 4 minutes, garnish the mussel gravy with basil leaves.
10. Serve immediately.

CRUSTY GRILLED MUSSELS

There is yet another way to enjoy the plain mussels with a crispy touch by grilling with breadcrumbs and garlic parsley butter on top. With nothing but herbs and lemon zest, these mussels are seasoned to get a fine taste.

| **Preparation time:** 05 minutes | **Cooking time:** 10 minutes | **Allergens:** wheat |

INGREDIENTS
- 1 lb. mussel, rinsed and debearded
- 1 cup toasted breadcrumb
- zest 1 lemon
- 2 tablespoons garlic and parsley butter
- Chopped tomato to garnish
- Fresh herbs to garnish

INSTRUCTIONS
1. Cook water to a boil in a large pot and place mussels in it for 3 mins.
2. This will let the mussels to open up, discard any if not opened.
3. Now, prepare and preheat the grill.
4. Mix zest with crumbs in a shallow bowl.
5. Remove the top shell from the mussels and drizzle butter on top.
6. Arrange these mussels in the baking sheet with their shell side down.
7. Top the mussels with crumbs mixture and place them in the grill.
8. Cover the grill for 4 minutes and let them cook.
9. Garnish with parsley and tomato.
10. Serve immediately.

NUTRITION FACTS

Serving 2		
Amount per serving		
Calories		510
		% Daily Value*
Total Fat	19.5g	25%
Saturated Fat	8.9g	45%
Cholesterol	94mg	31%
Sodium	1126mg	49%
Total Carbohydrate	47.3g	17%
Dietary Fiber	2.4g	9%
Total Sugars	3.4g	
Protein	34.3g	
Vitamin D	8mcg	40%
Calcium	161mg	12%
Iron	12mg	64%
Potassium	835mg	18%

SEAFOOD GARLIC COUSCOUS

When you pair a seafood mix, including fish, scallops, and chives with a freshly cooked couscous, your platter instantly turns into a health booster. This combination is good for all the special diet and health plans.

Preparation time: 10 minutes	**Cooking time:** 20 minutes	**Allergens:**

NUTRITION FACTS

Serving 4	
Amount per serving	
Calories	476
	% Daily Value*
Total Fat 9g	12%
Saturated Fat 1.4g	7%
Cholesterol 138mg	46%
Sodium 294mg	13%
Total Carbohydrate 68g	25%
Dietary Fiber 4.9g	17%
Total Sugars 0.8g	
Protein 32.9g	
Vitamin D 0mcg	0%
Calcium 110mg	8%
Iron 2mg	11%
Potassium 506mg	11%

INGREDIENTS

- 1 lb. codfish, cut into 1-inch pieces
- ½ lb. raw shrimp, peeled, deveined, and coarsely chopped
- ½ lb. bay scallops
- 4 scallions, sliced
- ½ cup chopped fresh chives
- ½ cup chopped fresh parsley
- salt and freshly ground pepper to taste
- 2 tbs. olive oil
- hot sauce to taste (optional)
- 2 (5.4-oz.) boxes garlic-flavored couscous

INSTRUCTIONS

1. Toss shrimp with scallions, codfish, scallops, chives, parsley, salt and pepper in a suitable bowl.
2. Take a deep wok or pan and preheat oil in it.
3. Stir in the seafood mixture prepared before.
4. Sauté this mixture until it turns golden in color.
5. Stir in hot sauce then dial down the heat to low.
6. Cover the seafood mixture with a lid.
7. Boil the couscous in water as per the instructions on its packet.
8. Drain and divide the cooked couscous into the serving plates.
9. Divide the fish mixture into the plates.
10. Serve immediately.

LOBSTER RICE PAELLA

Lobster's tail meat has this amazing taste of its own which is nicely complemented when cooked and served with rice paella. The short grain rice of this recipe is cooked in with tomato, saffron threads, and green beans.

| **Preparation Time:** 15 Minutes | **Cooking Time:** 25 minutes | **Allergens:** |

INGREDIENTS

- 2 small lobster tails
- 1 small onion, chopped
- 1 cup Spanish rice or short grain rice, soaked overnight, drained
- 2 garlic cloves, chopped
- 1 large pinch of Spanish saffron threads soaked in ½ cup water
- 1/2 teaspoon Sweet Spanish paprika
- 1/2 teaspoon cayenne pepper
- 1 1/2 tablespoons Olive Oil
- 1/4 teaspoon Aleppo pepper flakes
- 1 large Roma tomato, finely chopped
- 3 oz. French green beans
- 1/2 lb. prawns or shrimp, peeled and deveined
- ¼ cup fresh parsley, chopped
- Salt to taste
- water

INSTRUCTIONS

1. Pour about 3 cups of water in a large enough pot and boil it.
2. Place the lobster in this water for 2 minutes then immediately transfer to an ice bath.
3. Remove the meat from its shell and dice it into small size chunks.
4. Take a suitable skillet and preheat 3 tbsp oil in it.
5. Add onion, sauté for 2 minutes.
6. Stir in all the rice and cook for 3 minutes more while stirring.
7. Toss in garlic and pour in lobsters cooking liquid.
8. Stir in paprika, salt, peppers and saffron.
9. Add green beans and tomatoes then boil the ingredient in the liquid.
10. Cover this soupy mixture with a lid and reduce its heat to low.
11. Let it cook for 20 minutes on this temperature.
12. After removing the lid, place shrimp over the cooked rice.
13. Cover this rice again and let it all cook for 15 minutes.

NUTRITION FACTS

Servings: 2	
Amount per serving Calories	464
	% Daily Value*
Total Fat 13.1g	17%
Saturated Fat 2.2g	11%
Cholesterol 239mg	80%
Sodium 1013mg	44%
Total Carbohydrate 40.3g	15%
Dietary Fiber 3.8g	14%
Total Sugars 4.7g	
Protein 30.4g	
Vitamin D 0mcg	0%
Calcium 149mg	11%
Iron 3mg	16%
Potassium 630mg	13%

FISH AND VEGETABLE PARCELS

Unlike simple fish packets or grilled smoked fillets, these parcels have many of the extra secret ingredients including capers, olives, and potatoes. Whereas for seasoning there is lemon juice, zest, and herbs to add a mild yet refreshing taste to the fish.

Preparation time: 10 minutes	**Cooking time:** 25 minutes	**Allergens:**

INGREDIENTS

- 1 1/4 cup baby new potato, scrubbed
- 1 teaspoon olive oil
- 2 x 6oz firm white fish fillets, such as haddock or whiting
- 2 teaspoons sun-dried tomato paste or tomato purée
- finely grated zest of 1 small lemon
- 2 teaspoons lemon juice
- 10 black or green olives
- 1 tablespoon capers, rinsed
- 2 sprigs of fresh rosemary

INSTRUCTIONS

1. Let your oven preheat at 325° F (163° C).
2. Boil salt mixed water in a large pot and cook potatoes in this water for 12 minutes.
3. Place potatoes in a colander to cool to drain well.
4. Spread two 30 cm square shaped foil sheets and spray them with cooking oil.
5. Carefully place one fish fillet in each of the greased foil sheets.
6. Drizzle tomato paste, lemon juice, seasonings and lemon zest over the fillets.
7. Surround each fillet with capers, potatoes, and olives.
8. Place the sprigs of rosemary or thyme over the fillets then wrap them.
9. Place the fish parcels in the baking dish and bake them for 25 minutes in the preheated oven.
10. Allow the parcels to cool for 5 minutes, let the steam release out of the parcels.
11. Serve immediately.

NUTRITION FACTS

Serving 2		
Amount per serving		
Calories		314
		% Daily Value*
Total Fat	16.5g	21%
Saturated Fat	3.3g	17%
Cholesterol	31mg	10%
Sodium	998mg	43%
Total Carbohydrate	29g	11%
Dietary Fiber	3.8g	17%
Total Sugars	2.7g	
Protein	15.2g	
Vitamin D	0mcg	0%
Calcium	62mg	5%
Iron	4mg	24%
Potassium	659mg	14%

SEAFOOD WITH COUSCOUS SALAD

The best part about this seafood recipe is that the cooked fish is served with vegetable mixed couscous salad. The white fish fillets are simply seasoned with basil, lemon and chilis then they are simply baked.

Preparation time: 15 minutes	**Cooking time:** 20 minutes	**Allergens:**

INGREDIENTS

- 2 white fish fillets
- 2 lemons, zest and juice 1, the other cut into wedges
- 1 red chili, half sliced, half finely chopped
- 1 small bunch basil, shredded
- 7 oz. cherry tomatoes
- 4oz. couscous
- 2 tablespoons balsamic vinegar
- ½ cucumber, diced
- 2 tablespoons pitted black olives, halved

INSTRUCTIONS

1. Let your oven preheat at 375° F (191° C).
2. Take a foil sheet of small size and place the fish in it.
3. Add basil, seasonings, half of the lemon juice and zest and sliced chilies over the fish.
4. Surround the fillet with tomatoes then wrap it all by covering with another sheet.
5. Use the remaining fish and ingredients to make another parcel.
6. Place both the parcels in the baking sheet.
7. Let these parcels bake for 18 minutes in the preheated oven.
8. During this time, soak the couscous in boiled water for 15 minutes.
9. Drain the couscous and toss it with cucumber, basil, lemon zest, juice, olives, and tomatoes in a bowl.
10. Serve the baked fish with the couscous mixture.
11. Enjoy.

NUTRITION FACTS

Serving 2		
Amount per serving		
Calories		538
		% Daily Value*
Total Fat	13.3g	17%
Saturated Fat	2.1g	10%
Cholesterol	119mg	40%
Sodium	188mg	8%
Total Carbohydrate	56.8g	21%
Dietary Fiber	6.4g	23%
Total Sugars	5.5g	
Protein	47.1g	
Vitamin D	0mcg	0%
Calcium	112mg	9%
Iron	3mg	14%
Potassium	1165mg	25%

SAFFRON FISH GRATINS

The gratin is usually a cheese rich, crumbly bake. Here it is made using a saffron fish prawn mixture. once the seafood mixture is well cooked, it is transferred to a baking dish and topped with the crumbs, cheese, and parsley. It is then baked well to a nice melt.

Preparation Time: 05 Minutes	**Cooking Time:** 40 minutes	**Allergens:** Wheat, Dairy

INGREDIENTS

- 3 tablespoons olive oil
- 1 large onion, thinly sliced
- 1 fennel bulb (about 1 1/4 cup/9oz), trimmed and thinly sliced
- 3 large garlic cloves, finely sliced
- 1 heaped teaspoon coriander seeds, lightly crushed
- 1/2 cup white wine
- 2 x 14 oz. cans chopped tomatoes with herbs
- 2 tablespoons tomato purée
- a good pinch of saffron
- 1 bay leaf
- 1 tablespoon lemon juice
- 1 bunch parsley, leaves roughly chopped
- 2 lbs. mixed skinless fish fillets, cut into chunks
- 1 3/4 cups raw peeled king prawn
- ¼ cup finely grated parmesan
- 1/4 cup panko or coarse dried breadcrumbs
- green salad, to serve (optional)

INSTRUCTIONS

1. Preheat oil in a large nonstick pan.
2. Sauté fennel, garlic, onion and coriander seeds in it for 15 minutes.
3. Pour in wine, tomatoes, saffron, bay leaf, and tomato puree.
4. Adjust seasoning and cook for 15 minutes with occasional stirring.
5. Set the oven to 375° F (191° C).
6. Add lemon juice, parsley to the tomatoes mixture.
7. Place prawns and fish pieces into the sauce.
8. Cover the fish pan and let it cook for 5 minutes.
9. Transfer the fish and prawns along with sauce to a baking dish.
10. Toss breadcrumbs with cheese, parsley, and black pepper.
11. Spread this mixture over the fish and sauce.
12. Bake it for 20 minutes.
13. Serve.

NUTRITION FACTS

Servings: 6	
Amount per serving Calories	501
	% Daily Value*
Total Fat 26.4g	34%
Saturated Fat 5.5g	28%
Cholesterol 52mg	17%
Sodium 880mg	38%
Total Carbohydrate 38.7g	14%
Dietary Fiber 3.8g	13%
Total Sugars 3.8g	
Protein 27.5g	
Vitamin D 0mcg	0%
Calcium 85mg	7%
Iron 4mg	24%
Potassium 925mg	20%

BEANS RECIPES

- Spinach Bean
- Meatballs Chickpea Medley
- Black Beans Feta Salad
- Chickpeas Pepper Salad
- Juicy Red Bean Salad
- Basil Butter Beans
- Citrus Garlic Beans
- Greek StockBeans
- Meatball Beans Stew

THE COMPLETE MEDITERRANEAN COOKBOOK 2019 EDITION

SPINACH BEANS

Artichoke is a vegetable known for its succulent texture, and when it is cooked with beans and spinach mixture, it creates a combination worthy of adding to your Mediterranean menu. This beans recipe is a perfect luncheon for any day.

Preparation time: 10 minutes	**Cooking time:** 20 minutes	**Allergens:** Gluten

INGREDIENTS

- 1 tablespoon olive oil
- 1 small onion, chopped
- 2 garlic cloves, minced
- 1 can (14-1/2 ounces) diced tomatoes, undrained
- 2 tablespoons Worcestershire sauce
- 1/4 teaspoon salt
- 1/4 teaspoon pepper
- 1/8 teaspoon crushed red pepper flakes
- 1 can (15 ounces) cannellini beans, rinsed and drained
- 14 ounces, bacon chopped
- 6 ounces fresh baby spinach

NUTRITION FACTS

Serving 2		
Amount per serving		
Calories		475
		% Daily Value*
Total Fat	8.5g	11%
Saturated Fat	1.2g	6%
Cholesterol	0mg	0%
Sodium	628mg	27%
Total Carbohydrate	77.8g	28%
Dietary Fiber	31.1g	111%
Total Sugars	10.1g	
Protein	28.2g	
Vitamin D	0mcg	0%
Calcium	275mg	21%
Iron	11mg	63%
Potassium	2350mg	50%

INSTRUCTIONS

1. Use a suitable skillet to preheat cooking oil in it.
2. Saute bacon at first until it turn brown in color.
3. Stir in onion, sauté for 5 mins at most.
4. Then add garlic to the pan, cook for a minute.
5. Add Worcestershire sauce, seasonings, and tomatoes.
6. After boiling this mixture dial down its heat.
7. Cook the mixture for another 8 mins.
8. Toss in beans, and spinach,
9. Cook for 5 mins only until spinach is wilted.
10. Stir gently and serve immediately.

MEATBALLS CHICKPEA MEDLEY

BEANS RECIPES

This chickpea medley has all the essential ingredients of a Mediterranean diet including the meatballs, tomatoes, feta cheese and of course the chickpeas. The meatballs are served over the chickpea's mixture.

| **Preparation time:** 05 minutes | **Cooking time:** 20 minutes | **Allergens:** Egg, wheat, Dairy |

INGREDIENTS

- 2 egg whites
- 1/4 cup whole wheat panko breadcrumbs
- 1/4 cup fat-free feta cheese, crumbled
- 1/4 cup fresh parsley, chopped
- 2 tablespoons fresh rosemary, chopped
- 1-pound ground chicken
- 1 tablespoon olive oil
- 3 garlic cloves, roughly chopped
- 1/2 teaspoon kosher salt
- 1 cup grape or cherry tomatoes
- 1 (15 ounces) can chickpeas, drained

NUTRITION FACTS

Serving 6		
Amount per serving		
Calories		473
		% Daily Value*
Total Fat	13.9g	18%
Saturated Fat	3.3g	17%
Cholesterol	73mg	24%
Sodium	363mg	16%
Total Carbohydrate	49.6g	18%
Dietary Fiber	13.4g	48%
Total Sugars	10.1g	
Protein	38.5g	
Vitamin D	0mcg	0%
Calcium	140mg	11%
Iron	6mg	34%
Potassium	885mg	19%

INSTRUCTIONS

1. Let your oven preheat at 400° F (204° C).
2. Drizzle cooking oil in a baking sheet and brush it well to coat.
3. Beat egg white in a bowl along with parsley, panko, chicken ground, feta, and rosemary.
4. Toss chickpeas with salt, olive oil, garlic and tomatoes in a separate bowl.
5. First spread the chickpea mixture in the greased baking sheet.
6. Use the chicken mince mixture to make 2-inch balls.
7. Place these balls over the chickpeas and bake them for 20 mins in the oven.
8. Serve immediately.

THE COMPLETE MEDITERRANEAN COOKBOOK 2019 EDITION

BLACK BEANS FETA SALAD

Salads with balanced nutritional values are bliss for everyone, such as this black bean salad which is simply made out of canned beans tossed with tomatoes, dill, onion, and feta cheese.

Preparation time: 05 minutes | **Cooking time:** 0 minutes | **Allergens:** Gluten, Dairy

INGREDIENTS

- 4 Roma or plum tomatoes, chopped
- Two 14.5-ounce cans black beans, drained
- 1/2 red onion, sliced
- 1/4 cup fresh dill, chopped
- Juice of 1 lemon
- 2 tablespoons extra-virgin olive oil
- 1/4 cup crumbled feta cheese
- Salt to taste

INSTRUCTIONS

1. Add everything to a suitably sized bowl.
2. Reserve the feta and salt to garnish the beans salad.
3. Drizzle feta and salt on top of the salad.
4. Serve immediately.

NUTRITION FACTS

Serving 2		
Amount per serving		
Calories		362
		% Daily Value*
Total Fat	19.8g	25%
Saturated Fat	4.9g	24%
Cholesterol	17mg	6%
Sodium	265mg	12%
Total Carbohydrate	38.2g	14%
Dietary Fiber	11.1g	40%
Total Sugars	12.8g	
Protein	14.1g	
Vitamin D	0mcg	0%
Calcium	259mg	20%
Iron	6mg	33%
Potassium	1022mg	22%

Chickpeas Pepper Salad

Toss the chickpeas with onion, baked bell pepper, and tomato flesh to make this chickpeas salad in no time. this salad is both good for the side meal or the lunchtime entrees. Serve with your favorite sauce or garnishing on top.

Preparation time: 05 minutes	Cooking time: 25 minutes	Allergens: Gluten

Ingredients

- 1 red bell pepper, diced
- 2 cups of water
- 4 sun-dried tomatoes
- 1/4 cup red wine vinegar
- 2 garlic cloves, chopped
- 2 tablespoons extra-virgin olive oil
- Two 14.5-ounce cans chickpeas drained and rinsed
- 1/2 cup parsley, chopped
- Salt to taste

Instructions

1. Spread the red bell pepper slices in a baking tray their skin side up.
2. Bake the peppers for 8 mins in a preheated oven at 350° F (177° C).
3. Transfer the baked pepper to a ziplock bag.
4. Zip the bag and let it sit for 10 minutes then thinly slice the pepper.
5. Pour 2 cup water to a suitable bowl and heat it in the microwave for 4 mins.
6. Soak sun-dried tomatoes to the hot water and let it sit for 10 mins.
7. Drain these tomatoes and slice them thinly.
8. Toss garlic with olive oil and red wine vinegar in a bowl.
9. Add sliced bell pepper, parsley, chickpeas, and sun-dried tomatoes.
10. Add salt to season the mixture.
11. Serve immediately.

Nutrition Facts

Serving 2		
Amount per serving		
Calories		319
		% Daily Value*
Total Fat	15.8g	20%
Saturated Fat	2.1g	10%
Cholesterol	0mg	0%
Sodium	251mg	11%
Total Carbohydrate	38.3g	14%
Dietary Fiber	4.3g	15%
Total Sugars	15.8g	
Protein	9.4g	
Vitamin D	0mcg	0%
Calcium	67mg	5%
Iron	8mg	44%
Potassium	814mg	17%

JUICY RED BEAN SALAD

Kidney beans are known for thier good nutritional value, so a salad made out of them is surely a healthy meal. with the beets added to the mildly flavored beans, this salad gives you immense energy and fibers.

| **Preparation time:** 10 minutes | **Cooking time:** 10 minutes | **Allergens:** Dairy |

INGREDIENTS

- 4 beets, scrubbed and stems removed
- One 14.5-ounce can kidney beans, drained
- 4 green onions, chopped
- Juice of 1 lemon
- 2 tablespoons olive oil
- 1 tablespoon pomegranate juice
- Salt and pepper to taste
- Feta cheese to garnish
- Fresh greens, to garnish

INSTRUCTIONS

1. Boil 2 quarts water in a stockpot and add beets.
2. Then cook these beets for 10 minutes on a simmer.
3. Once done, strain them and transfer to an ice bath for 3 min approximately.
4. Peel these beets and slice them into half circled slices.
5. Toss kidney beans with green onion, olive oil, lemon juice, and pomegranate syrup in a bowl.
6. Add the sliced beets along with salt and pepper for seasoning.
7. Garnish with feta, greens and as desired.
8. Mix well then serve fresh.

NUTRITION FACTS

Serving 2		
Amount per serving		
Calories		373
		% Daily Value*
Total Fat	14.9g	19%
Saturated Fat	2.2g	11%
Cholesterol	0mg	0%
Sodium	491mg	21%
Total Carbohydrate	54g	20%
Dietary Fiber	12.4g	44%
Total Sugars	28.5g	
Protein	11.6g	
Vitamin D	0mcg	0%
Calcium	91mg	7%
Iron	4mg	22%
Potassium	1180mg	25%

BASIL BUTTER BEANS

The soothing basil flavor is most prominent in this butter beans recipe which is cooked in a sweet and sugary tomato and garlic sauce. Serve these beans with boiled white rice or warm tortillas.

Preparation time: 10 minutes	**Cooking time:** 10 minutes	**Allergens:**

INGREDIENTS
- 1 tablespoon olive oil
- 4 garlic cloves, crushed
- 14 oz. tin chopped tomato
- 2 teaspoons sugar
- 2 x 14 oz. tins butter beans, rinsed and drained
- small bunch basil, chopped

NUTRITION FACTS

Serving 2		
Amount per serving		
Calories		242
		% Daily Value*
Total Fat	8.3g	11%
Saturated Fat	1.6g	8%
Cholesterol	0mg	0%
Sodium	551mg	24%
Total Carbohydrate	33.1g	12%
Dietary Fiber	7.6g	27%
Total Sugars	10.5g	
Protein	9.1g	
Vitamin D	0mcg	0%
Calcium	92mg	7%
Iron	3mg	16%
Potassium	24mg	1%

INSTRUCTIONS
1. take a suitable size pan and heat cooking oil in it.
2. Stir in garlic and sauté for a minute.
3. Add sugar and tomatoes, seasoning, beans and a splash of water.
4. Cover this beans mixture and let it cook for 5 minutes.
5. Use basil to garnish the beans.
6. Serve warm.

CITRUS GARLIC BEANS

This recipe gives you a quick and easy mix of beans with basic and simple seasoning. The zesty and juicy butter beans are seasoned nothing with fresh garlic, parsley, and olive oil. That is why it is an anytime anywhere meal.

Preparation time: 10 minutes	Cooking time: 15 minutes	Allergens:

INGREDIENTS
- 1 tablespoon olive oil
- 1 large onion, sliced
- 1 garlic clove, crushed
- 2 x 14 oz./14oz can beans, rinsed and drained
- zest and juice 1 lemon
- 1 large bunch parsley, chopped

INSTRUCTIONS
1. Take a suitably sized cooking pan and preheat oil in it.
2. Add onion to sauté for 15 minutes until it is soft.
3. Stir in all the beans and garlic.
4. Cook enough to thoroughly the beans mixture.
5. Add in lemon zest, and lemon juice.
6. Use parsley to garnish.
7. Serve warm to enjoy.

NUTRITION FACTS

Serving 2		
Amount per serving		
Calories		212
		% Daily Value*
Total Fat	8.1g	10%
Saturated Fat	1.5g	7%
Cholesterol	0mg	0%
Sodium	533mg	23%
Total Carbohydrate	27.5g	10%
Dietary Fiber	6.7g	24%
Total Sugars	3.2g	
Protein	7.9g	
Vitamin D	0mcg	0%
Calcium	40mg	3%
Iron	1mg	5%
Potassium	116mg	2%

GREEK STOCK BEANS

In this recipe, the beans are cooked on a simmer in the mixture of tomato puree and stock, the slow simmering infused strong and deeper flavors into the beans. Use a fresh herb to garnish the cooked beans.

Preparation time: 10 minutes	**Cooking time:** 25 minutes	**Allergens:** Dairy

INGREDIENTS

- 1 large onion, chopped
- 2 tablespoons tomato purée
- small bunch dill, most chopped
- 1 tablespoon red wine vinegar
- 2 cups chicken stock
- 2 x 14 oz. can Gigante or butter beans, drained
- 2 tablespoons crumbled feta cheese

INSTRUCTIONS

1. Let a skillet preheat with oil on medium heat.
2. Stir garlic, onion, and seasonings saute it for 8mins.
3. Add tomato puree, beans, vinegar, stock and dill to the pan.
4. Let it simmer for 15mins until the cooking liquid is reduced.
5. Garnish with dill leaves and feta cheese.
6. Serve warm to enjoy.

NUTRITION FACTS

Serving 2		
Amount per serving		
Calories		256
		% Daily Value*
Total Fat	4.1g	5%
Saturated Fat	1.9g	9%
Cholesterol	8mg	3%
Sodium	900mg	39%
Total Carbohydrate	42.7g	16%
Dietary Fiber	9.9g	35%
Total Sugars	8.6g	
Protein	14.2g	
Vitamin D	0mcg	0%
Calcium	137mg	11%
Iron	6mg	32%
Potassium	1026mg	22%

MEATBALL BEANS STEW

BEANS RECIPES

Plain meatball stews do not taste as delicious as the beans mixed ones. This stew is loved for its chunky and crunchy texture where meatballs are served with deliciously cooked butter beans.

Preparation time: 05 minutes	**Cooking time:** 30 minutes	**Allergens:**

INGREDIENTS

- 1 3/4 cups lean pork mince
- 2 teaspoons olive oil
- 1 large red onion, chopped
- 2 peppers, sliced,
- 3 garlic cloves, crushed
- 1 tablespoon sweet smoked paprika
- 2 x 14 oz. cans chopped tomatoes
- 14 oz. can butter beans, drained
- 2 teaspoons golden caster sugar
- small bunch parsley, chopped
- crusty bread, to serve (optional

INSTRUCTIONS

1. Combine the minced pork with seasoning in a suitable ball.
2. Make small meatballs out of this mixture and keep them aside.
3. Add oil to a suitably sized pan and preheat it.
4. Toss the meatballs into the pan and sear them for 3 minutes per side until golden.
5. Push aside these meatballs, then stir in peppers and onions.
6. Stir cook for 5 minutes then add garlic and paprika.
7. Saute for a minute then stir in tomatoes.
8. Cover this sauce mixture with a lid and let it simmer for 10 mins.
9. Uncover the sauce then add seasoning, beans, and sugar.
10. Again simmer it for 10 minutes, then garnish with parsley and bread.
11. Serve immediately.

NUTRITION FACTS

Serving 2		
Amount per serving		
Calories		315
		% Daily Value*
Total Fat	11.3g	15%
Saturated Fat	0.9g	5%
Cholesterol	0mg	0%
Sodium	20mg	1%
Total Carbohydrate	37.2g	14%
Dietary Fiber	8.4g	30%
Total Sugars	13.1g	
Protein	19.2g	
Vitamin D	0mcg	0%
Calcium	70mg	5%
Iron	3mg	18%
Potassium	920mg	20%

BEAN MASH WITH GRILLED VEGGIES

If you are not up for a whole bean's recipe, then a bean mash with grilled vegetables is a nice combination. The beans are cooked, seasoned and mashed. This mash is served with nicely grilled vegetables.

Preparation time: 10 minutes   **Cooking time:** 10 minutes   **Allergens:**

INGREDIENTS

- 1 red pepper, deseeded and quartered
- 1 aubergine, sliced lengthways
- 2 zucchinis, sliced lengthways
- 2 tablespoons olive oil For the mash
- 14 oz. can haricot bean, rinsed
- 1 garlic clove, crushed
- 1/2 cup vegetable stock
- 1 tablespoon chopped coriander
- Lemon wedges, to serve

NUTRITION FACTS

Serving 2		
Amount per serving		
Calories		372
		% Daily Value*
Total Fat	15.4g	20%
Saturated Fat	2.6g	13%
Cholesterol	0mg	0%
Sodium	206mg	9%
Total Carbohydrate	60.6g	22%
Dietary Fiber	32.1g	115%
Total Sugars	27.8g	
Protein	12.3g	
Vitamin D	0mcg	0%
Calcium	338mg	26%
Iron	4mg	23%
Potassium	1159mg	25%

INSTRUCTIONS

1. Prepare the grill by greasing its grilling grate and preheat it.
2. Arrange all the vegetables on the grates and grill them until golden from both the sides.
3. Meanwhile, cook beans with garlic in simmering stock for 10 minutes.
4. Now mash the beans in this mixture roughly with spoon or masher.
5. If the mixture turn out to be too thick, then add a splash of water.
6. Spread this beans mash in the serving plates.
7. Place the grilled vegetables over it.
8. Garnish the plate with lemon wedges, coriander, oil, and black pepper.
9. Serve immediately.

THE COMPLETE MEDITERRANEAN COOKBOOK 2019 EDITION

SIDE AND SNACKS

Mediterranean sardine salad

Niçoise toasts

Herbed Olives

Stuffed tomatoes

Aubergine & pepper salad

Crispy squid with capers

Spiced tortilla

Garlic bread pizzas

SIDE AND SNACKS

MEDITERRANEAN SARDINE SALAD

Sardine is great seafood, and when tossed in a refreshing salad it tastes amazing. Instead of plain sardines, it is made out of tomatoes dipped sardines. The flavors are further enhanced by olives and caper.

| **Preparation time:** 05 minutes | **Cooking time:** 0 minutes | **Allergens:** |

INGREDIENTS

- 3 oz. salad leaves
- handful black olives, roughly chopped
- 1 tablespoon caper, drained and diced
- 2 x 7oz. cans sardines in tomato sauce, drained and sauce reserved
- 1 tablespoon olive oil
- 1 tablespoon red wine vinegar

INSTRUCTIONS

1. First, divide the salad onto 4 plates.
2. Top the leaves with olives and capers.
3. Slice the sardines roughly and divide it between the plates.
4. Garnish with olive oil, vinegar and tomato sauce.
5. Enjoy.

NUTRITION FACTS

Serving 2		
Amount per serving		
Calories		249
		% Daily Value*
Total Fat	17.1g	22%
Saturated Fat	5g	25%
Cholesterol	80mg	27%
Sodium	619mg	27%
Total Carbohydrate	5.7g	2%
Dietary Fiber	2.1g	8%
Total Sugars	2.1g	
Protein	16.6g	
Vitamin D	0mcg	0%
Calcium	608mg	47%
Iron	4mg	22%
Potassium	80mg	2%

NIÇOISE TOASTS

These toasts are great to serve as party snacks; it has all the ingredients which can guarantee good taste as well as loads of nutrients. The baguette is sliced and baked with anchovies mixed topping.

Preparation Time: 10 Minutes	**Cooking Time:** 40 minutes	**Allergens:** Wheat

INGREDIENTS

- 1 x 3/4 cup part-baked baguette, cut into 24 circles
- 3 tablespoons extra virgin olive oil, plus a little extra to drizzle
- 6 anchovy fillets in olive oil, drained
- 2 garlic cloves, crushed
- ½ medium red onion, finely chopped
- 1 ½ cup chopped tomatoes
- 2 tablespoons tomato purée
- 2 tablespoons mini capers, drained
- ½ teaspoons chili flakes
- 12 pitted black olives. Ideally, Kalamata drained and halved
- 2 tablespoons finely grated parmesan
- baby basil leaves, to serve

INSTRUCTIONS

1. let your oven preheat at 375° F (190° C).
2. Spread the bread slices in the baking sheet and toss them with a tablespoon of oil
3. Bake these slices for 12 minutes in the preheated oven.
4. On the other hand, heat the rest of the oil in a nonstick skillet.
5. Stir in onion, garlic, and anchovies, saute for 4 minutes.
6. Add puree, tomatoes, caper and chili flakes.
7. Cook this mixture with occasional stirring.
8. Remove the saucy mixture from the heat.
9. Spoon out this mixture over the baked slices.
10. Divide half of the olives over each piece and top it with parmesan.
11. Cover the slices and refrigerate them overnight.
12. Now preheat the oven to 375° F (190° C).
13. Place the pizza toasts in the oven to bake for 8 minutes.
14. Garnish with basil leaves and enjoy.

NUTRITION FACTS

Servings: 4		
Amount per serving Calories		328
		% Daily Value*
Total Fat	23g	30%
Saturated Fat	3.6g	18%
Cholesterol	40mg	13%
Sodium	2154mg	94%
Total Carbohydrate	19.8g	7%
Dietary Fiber	2g	7%
Total Sugars	3.6g	
Protein	14.1g	
Vitamin D	0mcg	0%
Calcium	207mg	16%
Iron	2mg	9%
Potassium	211mg	4%

HERBED OLIVES

SIDE AND SNACKS

It always tastes amazing when any of your Mediterranean recipes are served with olives on top. How about an all olives snack? Well, you can also serve these herbed olives as a side meal and also as the snack.

Preparation time: 05 minutes	**Cooking time:** 0 minutes	**Allergens:**

INGREDIENTS

- 3 cups olives
- 2 teaspoons extra-virgin olive oil
- ⅛ teaspoon dried oregano
- ⅛ teaspoon dried basil
- 1 clove garlic, crushed
- Freshly ground pepper, to taste

NUTRITION FACTS

Serving 6		
Amount per serving		
Calories		93
		% Daily Value*
Total Fat	8.8g	11%
Saturated Fat	1.2g	6%
Cholesterol	0mg	0%
Sodium	586mg	25%
Total Carbohydrate	4.7g	2%
Dietary Fiber	2.4g	8%
Total Sugars	0g	
Protein	0.7g	
Vitamin D	0mcg	0%
Calcium	69mg	5%
Iron	2mg	14%
Potassium	19mg	0%

INSTRUCTIONS

1. Toss the olives with rest of the ingredients in a bowl.
2. Insert a toothpick into each olive.
3. Serve and enjoy.

SIDE AND SNACKS

STUFFED TOMATOES

Mozzarella stuffed tomatoes are a healthy side meal for all the festive dinners. Tomatoes are first scooped out and then stuffed with cheese, pesto, and basil. Serve these with bread slices.

Preparation time: 10 minutes	**Cooking time:** 20 minutes	**Allergens:** Wheat, Dairy

NUTRITION FACTS

Serving 6		
Amount per serving		
Calories		280
		% Daily Value*
Total Fat	14.6g	19%
Saturated Fat	4.2g	21%
Cholesterol	13mg	4%
Sodium	248mg	11%
Total Carbohydrate	30.9g	11%
Dietary Fiber	2.7g	8%
Total Sugars	6.7g	
Protein	8.5g	
Vitamin D	0mcg	0%
Calcium	74mg	6%
Iron	2mg	11%
Potassium	531mg	11%

INGREDIENTS

- 6 really big tomatoes
- 2 balls of mozzarella, sliced
- 12 basil leaves, fresh
- 4 pieces red peppers, cooked
- 2 tablespoons pesto or red pesto

INSTRUCTIONS

1. Let the oven preheat at 375° F (190° C).
2. Chop off the top of all the tomatoes and remove the seeds from inside.
3. Arrange the tomatoes bases in a baking sheet with their cut side up.
4. Add chopped mozzarella to the tomato bases and top it with red pepper and leaves.
5. Stuff the tomatoes with layers of these ingredients.
6. In the end, top each base with a dollop of pesto.
7. Cover the tomato bases with their chopped off tops.
8. Bake these tomatoes in the preheated oven for 20 minutes.
9. Serve immediately.

THE COMPLETE MEDITERRANEAN COOKBOOK 2019 EDITION

AUBERGINE & PEPPER SALAD

This salad is made out of grilled aubergine and roasted peppers. Both the vegetables after grilling in the griddle pan, are seasoned with garlic and thyme. Later they are baked with the garlic to get the aromatic flavors.

Preparation time: 05 minutes   **Cooking time:** 30 minutes   **Allergens:**

INGREDIENTS

- 1 ¼ cup jar ready-roasted red pepper
- 2-3 aubergines
- olive oil
- 2 garlic cloves, sliced
- thyme leaves

INSTRUCTIONS

1. Place the roasted peppers in a colander to drain them.
2. Set the griddle pan over high heat.
3. Toss in the aubergines to the pan along with some oil.
4. Cook them for few minutes per sides until grilled.
5. Let your oven preheat at 325° F (163° C)
6. Add the grilled aubergines and peppers to a baking tray in rows.
7. Drizzle olive oil over these rows along with thyme leaves, seasoning and garlic slices.
8. Place the baking tray to the oven and bake for 30mins.
9. Serve immediately.

NUTRITION FACTS

Serving 2		
Amount per serving		
Calories		211
		% Daily Value*
Total Fat	1g	1%
Saturated Fat	0g	0%
Cholesterol	0mg	0%
Sodium	571mg	25%
Total Carbohydrate	43.2g	16%
Dietary Fiber	19.4g	69%
Total Sugars	16.5g	
Protein	7.6g	
Vitamin D	0mcg	0%
Calcium	75mg	6%
Iron	2mg	9%
Potassium	1267mg	27%

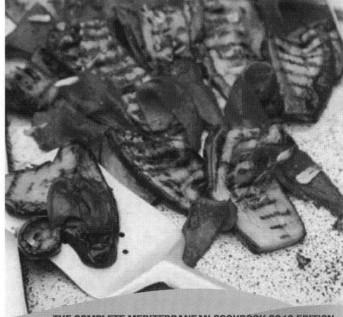

CRISPY SQUID WITH CAPERS

SIDE AND SNACKS

Having a crispy squid snack is as unique as it sounds. Squid has its distinct texture which complements the flour coating over it. Along with them, the capers are also coated and deep fried, so together they make a tempting delight.

| **Preparation time:** 05 minutes | **Cooking time:** 20 minutes | **Allergens:** wheat, egg |

INGREDIENTS

- 10 oz. baby squid, cleaned
- 7 oz. whole wheat flour
- 2 tablespoons caper, drained and finely chopped
- 1 garlic clove, crushed
- 5 tablespoons mayonnaise
- vegetable or sunflower oil, for frying
- lemon wedges, to serve

NUTRITION FACTS

Serving 2		
Amount per serving		
Calories		213
		% Daily Value*
Total Fat	5.1g	7%
Saturated Fat	0.8g	4%
Cholesterol	113mg	38%
Sodium	194mg	8%
Total Carbohydrate	29.9g	11%
Dietary Fiber	1g	4%
Total Sugars	0.9g	
Protein	11g	
Vitamin D	0mcg	0%
Calcium	24mg	2%
Iron	2mg	11%
Potassium	156mg	3%

INSTRUCTIONS

1. First, slice off the squid into thick rings.
2. Mix these rings with seasoning and flour in a shallow bowl.
3. Toss in capers to coat them as well.
4. Preheat oil in a wok for deep frying for capers and squid.
5. Once heated well, add the squid rings one by one after shaking off the excess flour.
6. Similarly, add the coated capers to the simmering oil.
7. When fried to a golden color, transfer the capers and squid to plate.
8. Soak excess oil by lining the plate with paper towel.
9. Serve them with garlic mayonnaise and lemon.

THE COMPLETE MEDITERRANEAN COOKBOOK 2019 EDITION

SPICED TORTILLA

Unlike the flour tortilla, this one is made out of the egg. A thin whisked and seasoned layer of egg is cooked in a pan, and then it is transferred to a grill where the strong smoky flavor is induced into the egg.

Preparation time: 05 minutes	Cooking time: 25 minutes	Allergens: Egg

INGREDIENTS

- 1 tablespoon sunflower oil
- 1 onion, sliced
- 1 red chili, deseeded and shredded
- 2 teaspoons curry spice
- 1 ½ cup cherry tomato
- 1 lb. cooked potato, sliced
- bunch coriander stalks finely chopped, leaves roughly chopped
- 8 eggs, beaten

INSTRUCTIONS

1. First, let the oil preheat in a suitable skillet.
2. Stir in half of the chili and onion to the pan and saute for 5mins.
3. Add the spices, tomatoes, potatoes and coriander stalks.
4. Beat the eggs with seasoning and pour it into the pan.
5. Cook the mixture for 10mins until it is set.
6. let your grill preheat and transfer the pan to this for 2mins.
7. Garnish it with remaining chilies and coriander leaves.
8. Slice and enjoy.

NUTRITION FACTS

Serving 4		
Amount per serving		
Calories		261
		% Daily Value*
Total Fat	12.5g	16%
Saturated Fat	3.1g	16%
Cholesterol	327mg	109%
Sodium	135mg	6%
Total Carbohydrate	24.3g	9%
Dietary Fiber	3.5g	12%
Total Sugars	2.8g	
Protein	14.1g	
Vitamin D	31mcg	154%
Calcium	67mg	5%
Iron	3mg	15%
Potassium	638mg	14%

GARLIC BREAD PIZZAS

SIDE AND SNACKS

Bread pizzas have always been a favorite snack for all occasions. The flour crust is topped with mozzarella mixed tomato and basil toppings. These pizzas are best to serve to all the vegetarians, and it makes an appealing delight for the dinner table.

Preparation time: 10 minutes	**Cooking time:** 15 minutes	**Allergens:** Wheat

INGREDIENTS

- 1 lb. strong whole wheat flour, plus extra for rolling
- 1 sachet fast-action yeast
- 1 teaspoon salt
- 2 tablespoons olive oi

For the topping
- 1/4 cup almond butter, softened
- 2 garlic cloves, crushed
- 1 ½ cup mozzarella, drained
- 4 tomatoes, roughly chopped
- handful basil leaves, roughly chopped
- 1 tablespoon extra-virgin olive oil
- 1 teaspoon balsamic vinegar

INSTRUCTIONS

1. Toss everything for dough base with 300 ml warm water in a suitable bowl.
2. Knead this dough well then cut them into eight equal pieces.
3. Roll out these pieces into 15 cm circles.
4. Place these pieces into a single large sheet or two medium baking sheets.
5. Stir garlic with melted butter in a mini bowl and pour over the dough.
6. Top these pieces with mozzarella then transfer them to the oven.
7. Bake the pizzas for 15 minutes in a preheated oven at 320° F (160° C)
8. Top the baked pizzas with remaining ingredients.
9. Serve immediately.

NUTRITION FACTS

Serving 4		
Amount per serving		
Calories		629
		% Daily Value*
Total Fat	21.8g	28%
Saturated Fat	9.6g	48%
Cholesterol	36mg	12%
Sodium	735mg	32%
Total Carbohydrate	92.2g	34%
Dietary Fiber	4.6g	16%
Total Sugars	3.6g	
Protein	16g	
Vitamin D	8mcg	40%
Calcium	43mg	3%
Iron	6mg	31%
Potassium	423mg	9%

Easy Tomato Pizzas

Tomato lovers will instantly fall for these mini pizzas as the crust is loaded with nothing but tomatoes and cheese. The crust is first layered with tomato sauce then with tomato slices and finally with cheese before baking.

Preparation time: 10 minutes	**Cooking time:** 12 minutes	**Allergens:** Wheat, Dairy

Ingredients

For the dough
- 1 lb. bread flour, plus more to dust
- 1 sachet fast-action yeast
- 2 tablespoons olive oil
- 1 1/2 cups warm water

For the topping
- 5 tablespoons roast tomato sauce
- 8 tomatoes
- Toppings: goat's cheese, grated Parmesan, handful rocket, prosciutto

Instructions

1. Mix yeast and 2 teaspoons with flour in a suitable bowl.
2. Pour in water and oil while stirring the mixture.
3. Knead this dough well for 2 minutes after setting it on rest for 5 mins.
4. Cover the dough with a plastic sheet and keep it at a warm place for 2 hours.
5. Let your oven preheat at 390° F (199° C)
6. Knead the dough into eight equal pieces and roll them into circles.
7. Place these circles into two baking sheets while keeping some distance in between.
8. Top each circle with a layer of sauce, tomato slices, parmesan, and seasoning.
9. Bake them for about 12 minutes in the preheated oven.
10. Enjoy.

Nutrition Facts

Serving 4		
Amount per serving		
Calories		522
		% Daily Value*
Total Fat	8.6g	11%
Saturated Fat	1.3g	6%
Cholesterol	0mg	0%
Sodium	115mg	5%
Total Carbohydrate	97.1g	35%
Dietary Fiber	6.3g	23%
Total Sugars	7.6g	
Protein	14.1g	
Vitamin D	0mcg	0%
Calcium	44mg	3%
Iron	6mg	34%
Potassium	768mg	16%

GOAT'S CHEESE PIZZA

This pizza is great to make at home and outside when you don't have enough to afford cooking or baking of any sort. So the sliced bread loaf is layered with pesto, grilled peppers, and goats cheese.

Preparation time: 10 minutes	**Cooking time:** 0 minutes	**Allergens:** Wheat, Dairy

INGREDIENTS

- 1 round focaccia loaf or long ciabatta
- 7 oz. marinated grilled red and yellow peppers in olive oil
- 3 tablespoons pesto
- 2/3 cup watercress
- 4oz. soft goat's cheese
- a handful of black olives

NUTRITION FACTS

Serving 4		
Amount per serving		
Calories		256
		% Daily Value*
Total Fat	12.2g	16%
Saturated Fat	5.2g	26%
Cholesterol	16mg	5%
Sodium	370mg	16%
Total Carbohydrate	28.7g	10%
Dietary Fiber	2g	7%
Total Sugars	2.5g	
Protein	10.6g	
Vitamin D	0mcg	0%
Calcium	84mg	6%
Iron	1mg	5%
Potassium	123mg	3%

INSTRUCTIONS

1. Slice the bread in half and set it aside.
2. Place the peppers in a colander to drain them while preserving their oil.
3. Top the bread pieces with a teaspoon of pesto over cut side.
4. Divide crumbled cheese, watercress, and pepper over each piece.
5. Use the remaining pesto and mix it with 1 tablespoon pepper oil.
6. Drizzle this oil over the slices.
7. Garnish with olives and serve.

VEGETARIAN RECIPES

Griddled vegetable & feta tart
Mediterranean gnocchi
Lemony mushroom & herb rice
Cashew Rice
Parmesan Roasted Broccoli
Baked Goat Cheese with Tomato Sauce
Roasted Vegetable Tabbouleh
Vegan Pesto Spaghetti Squash
Smoky Roasted Vegetables

VEGETARIAN RECIPES

GRIDDLED VEGETABLE & FETA TART

This is no ordinary vegetable tart, rather the phyllo sheet is baked with charred and grilled veggies, so the tart gets its smoky, strong taste which is complemented with the cheesy topping on top.

Preparation time: 10 minutes **Cooking time:** 30 minutes **Allergens:** Wheat, Dairy

INGREDIENTS

- 2 tablespoons olive oil
- 1 aubergine, sliced
- 2 zucchinis, sliced
- 2 red onions, cut into chunky wedges
- 3 large sheets filo pastry
- 10-12 cherry tomatoes, halved
- a drizzle of balsamic vinegar
- 1/2 cup feta cheese, crumbled
- 1 teaspoon dried oregano
- large bag mixed salad leaves and low-fat dressing, to serve

NUTRITION FACTS

Serving 4		
Amount per serving		
Calories		482
		% Daily Value*
Total Fat	26.5g	34%
Saturated Fat	12.5g	62%
Cholesterol	17mg	6%
Sodium	914mg	40%
Total Carbohydrate	50.8g	18%
Dietary Fiber	12.4g	44%
Total Sugars	22.6g	
Protein	14g	
Vitamin D	0mcg	0%
Calcium	167mg	13%
Iron	2mg	11%
Potassium	1346mg	29%

INSTRUCTIONS

1. Let your oven preheat at 375° F (190° C).
2. Pour 1 teaspoon oil into a griddle pan and heat over medium heat.
3. Toss in the aubergines and grill them until charred, then transfer them to a plate.
4. Then grill the zucchinis and onions, in the pan one after the other.
5. Grease a baking sheet with oil spread the layer of filo in it.
6. Spread the charred vegetables, tomatoes, and seasoning over the filo.
7. Drizzle feta, oregano and remaining oil over it.
8. Bake it for 20 minutes until golden from the top.
9. Slice and enjoy.

MEDITERRANEAN GNOCCHI

VEGETARIAN RECIPES

The soft and spongy gnocchi is cooked with charred and grilled vegetables. This flavorsome combination is flavored using red pesto, which tastes amazing when the recipe is served with fresh salad.

Preparation time: 10 minutes	**Cooking time:** 05 minutes	**Allergens:** Dairy

INGREDIENTS

- 14 oz. gnocchi
- 7 oz. chargrilled vegetables (peppers, aubergines, artichokes, and semi-dried tomatoes)
- 2 tablespoons red pesto
- a handful of basil leaves
- parmesan, to serve

INSTRUCTIONS

1. Boil gnocchi in salted water for 2 mins then instantly drain it.
2. Add the gnocchi to a pan along with splash water.
3. Toss in red pesto, charred vegetables, parmesan, and basil leaves.
4. Enjoy.

NUTRITION FACTS

Serving 4		
Amount per serving		
Calories		223
		% Daily Value*
Total Fat	4.5g	6%
Saturated Fat	0g	0%
Cholesterol	1mg	0%
Sodium	644mg	28%
Total Carbohydrate	38.6g	14%
Dietary Fiber	4.8g	17%
Total Sugars	1.6g	
Protein	5.6g	
Vitamin D	0mcg	0%
Calcium	30mg	2%
Iron	1mg	4%
Potassium	84mg	2%

VEGETARIAN RECIPES

LEMONY MUSHROOM & HERB RICE

No menu is complete without a good rice recipe. so this one is here to make your menu better. The rice is cooked with mushrooms and herbs. The mixture is served with chives and parsley when cooked and fluffed.

Preparation time: 10 minutes	**Cooking time:** 10 minutes	**Allergens:**

INGREDIENTS

- 1 cup long grain rice
- 1 1/4 cup pack chestnut mushrooms
- 2 tablespoons olive oil
- 2 large garlic cloves, finely chopped
- 5 tablespoons chopped parsley
- 3 tablespoons snipped chives
- finely grated zest 1 lemon

NUTRITION FACTS

Serving 4		
Amount per serving		
Calories		281
		% Daily Value*
Total Fat	8.9g	11%
Saturated Fat	1.4g	7%
Cholesterol	0mg	0%
Sodium	23mg	1%
Total Carbohydrate	43.6g	16%
Dietary Fiber	5.4g	19%
Total Sugars	0.8g	
Protein	9g	
Vitamin D	0mcg	0%
Calcium	78mg	6%
Iron	4mg	20%
Potassium	1436mg	31%

INSTRUCTIONS

1. Boil water with salt in a suitably sized pan.
2. Add rice to the water, cook them for 10mins with constant stirring.
3. When the rice is done, drain them through a sieve.
4. Dice the mushrooms and saute them in preheated oil for 4mins.
5. Stir in garlic, saute for a minute.
6. Toss in lemon zest, chives, parsley, and drained rice.
7. Enjoy.

THE COMPLETE MEDITERRANEAN COOKBOOK 2019 EDITION

CASHEW RICE

VEGETARIAN RECIPES

It's hard to imagine a fruity rice recipe, but this combination has made it all very real. Basmati rice is cooked with pepper and cashews, but the sauce used in this recipe is made out of mango sauce/ chutney, which is partly sweet and savory.

Preparation time: 10 minutes	**Cooking time:** 20 minutes	**Allergens:** Soy, cashews

INGREDIENTS

- 4oz. cashew nuts
- 3 cups cooked basmati rice, cooled
- 1 green pepper, deseeded and finely sliced
- 1 yellow pepper, deseeded and finely sliced
- 1 small red onion, finely sliced

For the dressing

- 3 tablespoons mango chutney
- 2 tablespoons light soy sauce
- 1 tablespoon oil
- 1 tablespoon brown sugar
- 2 teaspoons curry powder
- juice ½ lemon

INSTRUCTIONS

1. Toss all the ingredients for dressing in a suitable bowl.
2. Add cashews to a dry pan and toast them until golden brown.
3. Transfer these cashews to the mixed dressing.
4. Add rice, onions, and peppers.
5. Enjoy.

NUTRITION FACTS

Serving 4		
Amount per serving		
Calories		433
		% Daily Value*
Total Fat	17.1g	22%
Saturated Fat	3.2g	16%
Cholesterol	0mg	0%
Sodium	2384mg	104%
Total Carbohydrate	70.6g	26%
Dietary Fiber	2.5g	9%
Total Sugars	14.1g	
Protein	10.3g	
Vitamin D	0mcg	0%
Calcium	33mg	3%
Iron	4mg	24%
Potassium	391mg	8%

VEGETARIAN RECIPES

PARMESAN ROASTED BROCCOLI

The cheese parmesan broccoli bake is a nice option to serve the broccoli at your table for everyone. Due to basic seasonings and the cheese melt over its baked florets, the vegetables actually taste tempting.

Preparation time: 10 minutes	**Cooking time:** 25 minutes	**Allergens:** Dairy

INGREDIENTS

- 1-pound (16 ounces) broccoli florets, cut into bite-sized pieces
- 2 tablespoons olive oil
- Salt, to taste
- ½ cup grated Parmesan cheese
- 1 to 2 tablespoons thick balsamic vinegar
- Lemon zest from ½ to 1 lemon, preferably organic
- Pinch of red pepper flakes
- Pinch of flaky sea salt to salt

NUTRITION FACTS

Serving 4		
Amount per serving		
Calories		146
		% Daily Value*
Total Fat	10.4g	13%
Saturated Fat	3g	15%
Cholesterol	10mg	3%
Sodium	167mg	7%
Total Carbohydrate	8.5g	3%
Dietary Fiber	3g	11%
Total Sugars	2.4g	
Protein	7.7g	
Vitamin D	0mcg	0%
Calcium	178mg	14%
Iron	1mg	5%
Potassium	359mg	8%

INSTRUCTIONS

1. Let your oven preheat 400° F (204° C).
2. Spread a parchment paper in a baking sheet.
3. Season the broccoli florets with salt.
4. Spread the broccoli florets in the baking sheet.
5. First, bake the broccoli for 15 minutes in the heated oven.
6. Then drizzle parmesan cheese over after tossing them.
7. Bake these florets again for 10 mins.
8. Season them with salt, red pepper flakes, lemon zest, and balsamic vinegar.
9. Enjoy.

THE COMPLETE MEDITERRANEAN COOKBOOK 2019 EDITION

BAKED GOAT CHEESE WITH TOMATO SAUCE

VEGETARIAN RECIPES

If you call them little cheese cups, that would be any wrong. The ramekins are filled with well-cooked tomato sauce which is later topped with cheese. They are baked and served warm. You can add any other vegetable of your choice to make it more filling.

Preparation time: 5 minutes	**Cooking time:** 25 minutes	**Allergens:** Dairy

INGREDIENTS

- 1 tablespoon olive oil
- ½ cup finely chopped white onion
- 2 medium garlic cloves, pressed or minced
- 1 ¼ tablespoon chopped fresh basil
- ¼ teaspoon red pepper flakes
- ¼ teaspoon dried oregano
- 1 ½ teaspoon white wine vinegar
- 1 can (15 ounces) crushed tomatoes
- ½ teaspoon kosher salt or ¼ teaspoon fine sea salt
- Freshly ground black pepper
- 4 ounces goat cheese
- Whle grain baguette to serve

INSTRUCTIONS

1. Let your oven preheat at 375° F (190° C).
2. Pour in oil to a heating pan and saute onion in it for 3mins.
3. Toss in red pepper flakes, basil, oregano, and garlic.
4. Stir cook for a minute then drizzle in white wine vinegar.
5. Add salt, pepper, and tomatoes to the pan.
6. Cover the tomato mixture with a lid and cook it for 10mins on a simmer.
7. Divide this saucy mixture into the ramekins and top them with cheese.
8. Place the stuffed ramekins in a baking tray and bake for 15 mins in a preheated oven.
9. Try olive oil and basil for garnishing.
10. Enjoy with warm bread.

NUTRITION FACTS

Serving 4		
Amount per serving		
Calories		112
		% Daily Value*
Total Fat	10.4g	13%
Saturated Fat	3g	15%
Cholesterol	10mg	3%
Sodium	167mg	7%
Total Carbohydrate	8.5g	3%
Dietary Fiber	3g	11%
Total Sugars	2.4g	
Protein	7.7g	
Vitamin D	0mcg	0%
Calcium	178mg	14%
Iron	1mg	5%
Potassium	359mg	8%

THE COMPLETE MEDITERRANEAN COOKBOOK 2019 EDITION

ROASTED VEGETABLE TABBOULEH

Tabbouleh has quite a refreshing taste. the dish is full of fibers and all the essential nutrients. The boiled bulgur wheat is tossed with vegetables and the beans along with basic lemon peel dressing.

Preparation time: 10 minutes	**Cooking time:** 25 minutes	**Allergens:**

INGREDIENTS

- ¾ cup bulgur
- 3 medium carrots, chopped
- 1 small red onion, chopped
- Cooking spray
- 1 (16-ounce) can garbanzo beans, rinsed and drained
- ½ cup chopped fresh parsley
- ½ teaspoon finely shredded lemon peel
- 3 tablespoons lemon juice
- 2 tablespoons water
- 2 tablespoons olive oil
- 2 teaspoons snipped fresh thyme
- ¼ teaspoon ground black pepper
- ⅛ teaspoon salt
- 1 medium tomato, chopped

INSTRUCTIONS

1. Let your oven preheat at 400° F (204° C)
2. Boil the bulgur wheat in water as per the given instruction on the packet.
3. Drain the bulgur once done then keep it aside.
4. Spread carrots and onions pieces in a baking dish.
5. Toss these vegetables with olive oil then bake them for 25 minutes.
6. Mix bulgur with lemon peel, parsley, pepper, salt, lemon juice, garbanzo in a large bowl.
7. Toss in the baked vegetables.
8. Garnish and enjoy.

NUTRITION FACTS

Serving 4		
Amount per serving Calories		370
		% Daily Value*
Total Fat	10.6g	14%
Saturated Fat	1.5g	7%
Cholesterol	0mg	0%
Sodium	57mg	2%
Total Carbohydrate	58.7g	21%
Dietary Fiber	15.9g	57%
Total Sugars	9.6g	
Protein	14.1g	
Vitamin D	0mcg	0%
Calcium	105mg	8%
Iron	5mg	29%
Potassium	852mg	18%

VEGAN PESTO SPAGHETTI SQUASH

Spaghetti squash has always been a nice alternative to carb-rich pasta meal since it is made out of cooked squash. here the spaghetti from the squash is mixed with mushrooms tomato sauce along with basil and cashews.

| **Preparation time:** 10 minutes | **Cooking time:** 50 minutes | **Allergens:** Cashews |

INGREDIENTS

- 1 2½- to 3-pound spaghetti squash, halved lengthwise and seeded
- 4 tablespoons extra-virgin olive oil, divided
- 8 ounces cremini mushrooms, sliced
- ½ cup julienned sun-dried tomatoes
- ½ teaspoon salt, divided
- 1 cup packed fresh basil leaves
- 2 cloves garlic, coarsely chopped
- ⅓ cup unsalted raw cashews
- 3 tablespoons lemon juice
- 2 teaspoons nutritional yeast
- ½ teaspoon ground pepper

INSTRUCTIONS

1. Slice the squash in two halves and place them in the baking sheet.
2. Bake these halves in the preheated oven for 45 minutes at 400 degrees F.
3. Saute mushrooms, and tomatoes with salt in a tbsp oil for 5 minutes in a pan.
4. Blend 3 tbsp oil with basil, lemon juice, cashews, garlic, salt, yeast, and pepper.
5. Scrape the flesh of the baked squash to get thin spaghetti.
6. Place the spaghetti in a colander to drain all the liquid.
7. Divide the drained spaghetti into the serving plates.
8. Top them with mushrooms and basil sauce. Enjoy.

NUTRITION FACTS

Serving 4		
Amount per serving		
Calories		245
		% Daily Value*
Total Fat	20g	26%
Saturated Fat	3.3g	16%
Cholesterol	0mg	0%
Sodium	450mg	20%
Total Carbohydrate	15g	5%
Dietary Fiber	2.1g	7%
Total Sugars	4.4g	
Protein	5.4g	
Vitamin D	0mcg	0%
Calcium	41mg	3%
Iron	2mg	12%
Potassium	668mg	14%

VEGETARIAN RECIPES

CHARRED GREEN BEANS WITH MUSTARD

Green beans, when charred and grilled taste amazing. Further such beans are seasoned with pepper, salt, and mustard. The use of red wine vinegar adds an earthy taste to the beans. Serve them with chopped hazelnuts on top.

Preparation time: 10 minutes	**Cooking time:** 10 minutes	**Allergens:** Hazelnuts

INGREDIENTS
- 1-pound green beans, trimmed
- 3 tablespoons extra-virgin olive oil, divided
- 1 tablespoon red-wine vinegar
- 2 teaspoons whole-grain mustard
- ¼ teaspoon salt
- ¼ teaspoon ground pepper
- ¼ cup toasted chopped hazelnuts

NUTRITION FACTS

Serving 2		
Amount per serving		
Calories		315
		% Daily Value*
Total Fat	27.2g	35%
Saturated Fat	3.5g	17%
Cholesterol	0mg	0%
Sodium	328mg	14%
Total Carbohydrate	18.3g	7%
Dietary Fiber	8.7g	31%
Total Sugars	3.6g	
Protein	5.6g	
Vitamin D	0mcg	0%
Calcium	96mg	7%
Iron	3mg	16%
Potassium	544mg	12%

INSTRUCTIONS
1. Prepare and preheat the grill.
2. Toss green beans with a tablespoon oil in a bowl.
3. Grill the beans in the preheated grill for 7 minutes.
4. Season these beans with pepper, vinegar, mustard, salt, and oil.
5. Garnish the beans with hazelnuts.
6. Enjoy.

VEGETARIAN RECIPES

SMOKY ROASTED VEGETABLES

Let's make good use out of all the summer vegetables and layer them together in a colorful ratatouille to brighten up your dinner table. Thin slices of the vegetables are baked together with herbs.

Preparation time: 10 minutes	Cooking time: 1hr. 15 minutes	Allergens:

NUTRITION FACTS

Serving 4		
Amount per serving		
Calories		231
		% Daily Value*
Total Fat	17.5g	22%
Saturated Fat	2.5g	12%
Cholesterol	0mg	0%
Sodium	482mg	21%
Total Carbohydrate	19.6g	7%
Dietary Fiber	7.3g	26%
Total Sugars	10.6g	
Protein	3.6g	
Vitamin D	0mcg	0%
Calcium	59mg	5%
Iron	2mg	10%
Potassium	760mg	16%

INGREDIENTS

- 3 medium tomatoes, sliced
- 2 small red onions, sliced into rounds and separated
- 1 small eggplant, cut into 3-inch sticks
- 1 small orange bell pepper, sliced
- 1 small yellow bell pepper, sliced
- 1 small summer squash, cut into 3-inch sticks
- 1 small zucchini, cut into 3-inch sticks
- 1 teaspoon sea salt, divided
- 3 sprigs fresh parsley
- 2 sprigs fresh thyme
- 1 bay leaf
- 4 cloves garlic, divided
- ⅓ cup extra-virgin olive oil
- 1 tablespoon balsamic vinegar
- 1 tablespoon red-wine vinegar

INSTRUCTIONS

1. Let your oven preheat at 350° F (177° C)
2. Season the vegetables with salt by tossing them well in a bowl.
3. Place the vegetables in a baking dish, alternatively to form rainbow color rows.
4. Tie thyme, parsley and bay leave with a kitchen string.
5. Place these tied leaves at the center of the vegetables.
6. Top them with some oil and garlic cloves.
7. Bake the veggies for 1 hour and 15 minutes in the preheated oven.
8. Garnish with a drizzle of vinegar.
9. Enjoy.

THE COMPLETE MEDITERRANEAN COOKBOOK 2019 EDITION

DESSERT RECIPES

- Banana Greek Yogurt Bowl
- Popped Quinoa Bars
- Greek Baklava
- Orange Sesame Cookies
- Honey yogurt cheesecake
- Fruity Almond cake
- Almond Orange Pandoro
- Compote Dipped Berries Mix
- Honey Glazed Pears

BANANA GREEK YOGURT BOWL

These flaxseed yogurt bowls are great to serve both as after meal dessert or even as breakfast on the Mediterranean diet. these are relatively simple to make as you only need to bring everything together and does not involve cooking.

Preparation time: 10 minutes	**Cooking time:** 0 minutes	**Allergens:** Flaxseeds

INGREDIENTS

- 4 cups vanilla Greek yogurt
- 2 medium bananas sliced
- 1/4 cup creamy natural peanut butter
- 1/4 cup flax seed meal
- 1 teaspoon nutmeg

INSTRUCTIONS

1. Add yogurt to the serving bowls.
2. Stir in melted butter, flaxseeds, and nutmeg.
3. Top the yogurt with banana slices equally.
4. Enjoy.

NUTRITION FACTS

Serving 4		
Amount per serving		
Calories		414
		% Daily Value*
Total Fat	14.7g	19%
Saturated Fat	4.2g	21%
Cholesterol	20mg	7%
Sodium	143mg	6%
Total Carbohydrate	48.3g	18%
Dietary Fiber	4.5g	16%
Total Sugars	31.7g	
Protein	24.7g	
Vitamin D	0mcg	0%
Calcium	206mg	16%
Iron	4mg	20%
Potassium	715mg	15%

POPPED QUINOA BARS

Quinoa is a master grain of a healthy diet, so we can make good use of it by adding it to a chocolate bar. The melted ingredients are mixed with toasted quinoa, and then the bar is refrigerated until set. These bars are great for prolonged preservations.

Preparation time: 10 minutes	**Cooking time:** 0 minutes	**Allergens:**

INGREDIENTS

- 4 4oz semi-sweet chocolate bars, chopped
- 1 cup dry quinoa
- 1 tablespoon peanut butter
- ½ teaspoon vanilla

INSTRUCTIONS

1. Toast quinoa in a dry heated pan until it turns golden in color.
2. Stir in vanilla, melted chocolate, and peanut butter.
3. Once mixed well, spread this mixture in a baking sheet evenly.
4. Refrigerate them for 4 hours then break it into small pieces.
5. Enjoy.

NUTRITION FACTS

Serving 6		
Amount per serving		
Calories		278
		% Daily Value*
Total Fat	11.8g	15%
Saturated Fat	6.6g	33%
Cholesterol	7mg	2%
Sodium	37mg	2%
Total Carbohydrate	36.2g	13%
Dietary Fiber	3.1g	11%
Total Sugars	15.4g	
Protein	6.9g	
Vitamin D	0mcg	0%
Calcium	69mg	5%
Iron	2mg	12%
Potassium	286mg	6%

GREEK BAKLAVA

DESSERT RECIPES

Baklava is famous in several sub-cuisines. It is equally popular in Greece and turkey. The Greek baklava is made with layers of phyllo sheets layered with mildly sweet nuts paste. the syrup is later poured over baked layers for more taste.

Preparation time: 10 min	**Cooking time:** 55 min	**Allergens:** Walnuts, almonds, sesame

INGREDIENTS

- 12 sheets phyllo pastry dough
- 2 cups almonds, chopped
- 2 cups walnuts, chopped
- 1 cup sesame seeds
- 2 teaspoons ground cinnamon
- 1 teaspoon ground cloves
- 3 tablespoons honey
- 1 cup extra virgin olive oil

Syrup

- 2 cups of water
- 1 ¼ cup honey
- 1 cinnamon stick
- The peel of 1 lemon
- Juice of 1 lemon

INSTRUCTIONS

1. Let your oven preheat at 350° F (177° C)
2. Toss walnuts with cinnamon, almonds, sesame seeds, ground cloves, and honey in a bowl.
3. Brush both sides of each phyllo sheet with olive oil.
4. Place this layer in the baking dish, top it with 3 more oiled layers of phyllo sheets.
5. Pour in half of the nut mixture and evenly spread it.
6. Add the half of the nut mixture and spread it evenly.
7. Again add layers of 4 oiled phyllo sheets.
8. Pour the other half of the nut mixture on top and spread it.
9. Bake the baklawa for 35 minutes in the preheated oven.
10. Slice the layers into squares, and allow it to cool.
11. On the other hand, stir-cook all the sauce ingredients for 15 minutes on a simmer.
12. Pour it over the baklava pieces.
13. Enjoy.

NUTRITION FACTS

Serving 12		
Amount per serving		
Calories		651
		% Daily Value*
Total Fat	43.8g	56%
Saturated Fat	4.5g	23%
Cholesterol	0mg	0%
Sodium	149mg	6%
Total Carbohydrate	61.3g	22%
Dietary Fiber	5.6g	20%
Total Sugars	40.1g	
Protein	13g	
Vitamin D	0mcg	0%
Calcium	209mg	16%
Iron	4mg	22%
Potassium	288mg	6%

ORANGE SESAME COOKIES

These orange cookies are loved for their refreshing citrus flavor. The dough is both flavored with the orange and lemon juice. Cookies are liberally rolled in the sesame seeds and then baked which gives a nice aromatic flavor.

Preparation time: 10 minutes	**Cooking time:** 25 minutes	**Allergens:** wheat, sesame

NUTRITION FACTS

Serving 24		
Amount per serving		
Calories		375
		% Daily Value*
Total Fat	20.2g	26%
Saturated Fat	2.9g	14%
Cholesterol	0mg	0%
Sodium	109mg	5%
Total Carbohydrate	44.5g	16%
Dietary Fiber	1.9g	7%
Total Sugars	12.8g	
Protein	5.2g	
Vitamin D	0mcg	0%
Calcium	77mg	6%
Iron	3mg	16%
Potassium	111mg	2%

INGREDIENTS

- 2 cups extra virgin olive oil
- 2 cups brown sugar
- 1 cup orange juice, freshly squeezed
- Juice of 1 lemon
- 1 shot brandy
- 1 teaspoon ground cinnamon
- 1 teaspoon ground cloves
- 2 teaspoons baking soda
- 7 ½ cups whole wheat flour
- 1 cup sesame seed

INSTRUCTIONS

1. Let your oven preheat at 350° F (177° C)
2. Beat sugar with olive oil in an electric mixer for 10 mins until dissolved.
3. Add orange juice and beat again for 2 mins.
4. Stir in cinnamon, lemon juice, cloves, baking soda, and brandy.
5. Fold in the flour and mix well to prepare smooth cookie dough.
6. Make small cookies and roll them in sesame seeds.
7. Set these cookies in the baking tray.
8. Bake them for 25 mins in the preheated oven.
9. Enjoy.

HONEY YOGURT CHEESECAKE

DESSERT RECIPES

This cheesecake has the crispy biscuit crust and a jiggle yogurt and honey cheesecake filling. Once the cake is baked, the cake is topped with fresh fruits, which can include strawberries or berries.

| Preparation time: 10 minutes | Cooking time: 25 minutes | Allergens: Dairy |

INGREDIENTS

- 4oz. Amaretti biscuits
- 3 tablespoons, flaked almonds
- 3 tablespoons almond butter, melted
- 1 cup greek yogurt
- 26 oz. Mascarpone
- 2 eggs
- Zest from 1 lemon
- Zest from 1 orange
- 1 cup honey
- Fresh fruit, to serve

INSTRUCTIONS

1. Let your oven preheat at 280° F (138° C)
2. Seal almonds and biscuits to a ziplock bag. Crush them using a rolling pin.
3. Toss this mixture with crumbs and butter.
4. Spread this mixture to a baking dish evenly.
5. Bake it for 10mins in the preheated oven.
6. Whisk eggs in yogurt and mascarpone using a beater.
7. Stir in orange and lemon zest.
8. Add honey to flavor the batter then transfer the batter to the baked crust.
9. Cover the pan with a foil tent then bake it for one hour in the preheated oven.
10. Bake the pie for 15 mins in the preheated oven.
11. Garnish with honey and almonds.
12. Enjoy.

NUTRITION FACTS

Serving 8		
Amount per serving		
Calories		460
		% Daily Value*
Total Fat	22.9g	29%
Saturated Fat	11.3g	57%
Cholesterol	101mg	34%
Sodium	133mg	6%
Total Carbohydrate	50g	18%
Dietary Fiber	1.2g	4%
Total Sugars	36.4g	
Protein	16.8g	
Vitamin D	7mcg	34%
Calcium	240mg	18%
Iron	1mg	5%
Potassium	208mg	4%

THE COMPLETE MEDITERRANEAN COOKBOOK 2019 EDITION

DESSERT RECIPES

FRUITY ALMOND CAKE

For a chunky and soft cake bite, try this almond cake recipe which is ultra-spongy in texture yet the mixed dried fruits and almonds makes crunchy in taste. serve with almond garnishing.

Preparation time: 10 minutes	**Cooking time: 2** hours	**Allergens:** Almonds, wheat,

INGREDIENTS

- 2 lbs. bag mixed dried fruit
- Zest and juice from 2 large oranges
- 1/2 cup sherry
- 1 1/4 cup pack butter, softened, plus extra for the tin
- 1 1/4 cup light muscovado sugar
- seeds scraped from 1 vanilla pod
- 5oz. whole wheat flour
- 4oz. ground almond
- 2 teaspoons mixed spice
- 4 large eggs, beaten
- 5oz. whole almond

NUTRITION FACTS

Serving 8		
Amount per serving Calories	Calories	613
		% Daily Value*
Total Fat	41.8g	54%
Saturated Fat	19.8g	99%
Cholesterol	169mg	56%
Sodium	261mg	11%
Total Carbohydrate	54.1g	20%
Dietary Fiber	2.7g	10%
Total Sugars	36.8g	
Protein	9g	
Vitamin D	29mcg	143%
Calcium	72mg	6%
Iron	2mg	11%
Potassium	191mg	4%

INSTRUCTIONS

1. Toss fruits with orange juice, zest, and sherry.
2. Let the fruits soak in the juices in the refrigerator overnight.
3. Let the oven preheat at 280° F (138° C)
4. Take a cake pan and grease it with butter and spread brown paper in it.
5. Beat sugar and vanilla seeds in butter until smooth and creamy.
6. Add spices, flour, and almond ground, mix well until smooth.
7. Fold in marinated fruits and whole almonds.
8. Pour the batter in the baking dish and bake it for 1 hour 30 minutes.
9. Then reduce the temperature of the oven, to 250° F (121° C).
10. Bake again for 1 hour and 30 minutes.
11. Enjoy.

THE COMPLETE MEDITERRANEAN COOKBOOK 2019 EDITION

ALMOND ORANGE PANDORO

Pandoro cake or bread has a different shape, so the layers of its sliced stuffed with creamy and zest mixture along with almonds, make this dessert a unique serving for the table.

Preparation time: 10 minutes	**Cooking time:** 0	**Allergens:** Almonds, wheat, Dairy

INGREDIENTS

- 1 1/4 cups coconut cream
- 1 1/4 cup mascarpone
- 4 tablespoons sherry
- 1 large orange, zested
- 1 pandoro
- 1/4 cup almonds, whole

NUTRITION FACTS

Serving	6	Calories	346
			% Daily Value*
Total Fat	10.4g		13%
Saturated Fat	3g		15%
Cholesterol	10mg		3%
Sodium	167mg		7%
Total Carbohydrate	8.5g		3%
Dietary Fiber	3g		11%
Total Sugars	2.4g		
Protein	7.7g		
Vitamin D	0mcg		0%
Calcium	178mg		14%
Iron	1mg		5%
Potassium	359mg		8%

INSTRUCTIONS

1. Whisk cream with icing sugar, mascarpone, ¾ zest and half sherry in a suitable bowl.
2. Dice the pandoro into 5 equal sized horizontal slices.
3. Place the bottom slice in a plate and top them with remaining sherry.
4. Spoon the mascarpone mixture over the slice.
5. Add almonds on top and place another pandoro slice over.
6. Continue adding layers of pandoro slices and cream mixture.
7. Enjoy.

BLUEBERRY & MACADAMIA FLAPJACKS

DESSERT RECIPES

Flapjacks of all types and flavors sound delicious when you need a rich, crunchy dessert. Blueberry macadamia flapjacks are just another good way to enjoy oats, and nuts together with a buttery mix. Serve with white chocolate for best taste.

Preparation time: 10 minutes	**Cooking time:** 50 minutes	**Allergens:** Nuts, wheat

NUTRITION FACTS

Serving 6		
Amount per serving		
Calories		346
		% Daily Value*
Total Fat	20.6g	26%
Saturated Fat	12g	60%
Cholesterol	80mg	27%
Sodium	85mg	4%
Total Carbohydrate	16.5g	6%
Dietary Fiber	1.4g	5%
Total Sugars	9.5g	
Protein	8.6g	
Vitamin D	13mcg	65%
Calcium	153mg	12%
Iron	1mg	3%
Potassium	158mg	3%

INGREDIENTS

- 1 1/4 cup pack butter, plus extra for greasing
- 5oz. demerara sugar
- 3 tablespoons golden syrup
- 7 oz. porridge oats
- 5oz. jumbo rolled oats
- 5oz. macadamia nuts, roughly chopped
- zest from half lemon
- 3 tablespoons whole wheat flour
- 7 oz. blueberries
- 3 tablespoons white chocolate, finely chopped

INSTRUCTIONS

1. Let your oven preheat at 280° F (138° C)
2. Take a square pan with oil and layer it with wax paper.
3. Cook butter with a pinch of salt, golden syrup and sugar in a saucepan on low heat.
4. Toss the oats with nuts, lemon zest, and flour in a separate bowl.
5. Stir in the cooked butter mixture and mix well until smooth.
6. Fold in berries then spread the mixture to a baking pan.
7. Evenly spread it and bake it for 45 mins until golden in color.
8. Once done, allow the flapjack to cool at room temperature.
9. Meanwhile, melt the chocolate in the microwave on medium heat.
10. Drizzle this white chocolate over the flapjack.
11. Cut it into bite-size chunks.
12. Enjoy.

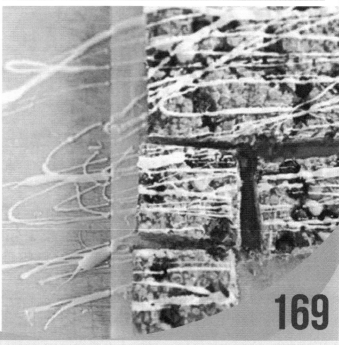

THE COMPLETE MEDITERRANEAN COOKBOOK 2019 EDITION

COMPOTE DIPPED BERRIES MIX

DESSERT RECIPES

Berry compotes are great to serve as desserts or to make more desserts out of it. this compote is served directly or used as a cheesecake topping. All berries are dipped into a sweet tea based, mint and orange infusion.

Preparation time: 10 minutes	**Cooking time:** 0 minutes	**Allergens:**

INGREDIENTS

- 1/2cup water
- 3 orange pekoe tea bags
- 3 4-inch sprigs fresh mint
- 1 cup fresh strawberries, hulled and halved lengthwise
- 1 cup fresh golden raspberries
- 1 cup fresh red raspberries
- 1 cup fresh blackberries
- 1 cup fresh blueberries
- 1 cup pitted, halved fresh sweet cherries
- 1 ml bottle Sauvignon Blanc
- ½ cup pomegranate juice
- 1 teaspoon vanilla
- Fresh mint sprigs

NUTRITION FACTS

Serving 6		
Amount per serving		
Calories		346
		% Daily Value*
Total Fat	20.6g	26%
Saturated Fat	12g	60%
Cholesterol	80mg	27%
Sodium	85mg	4%
Total Carbohydrate	16.5g	6%
Dietary Fiber	1.4g	5%
Total Sugars	9.5g	
Protein	8.6g	
Vitamin D	13mcg	65%
Calcium	153mg	12%
Iron	1mg	3%
Potassium	158mg	3%

INSTRUCTIONS

1. Soak 3 mint sprigs and tea bags in hot boiled water for 10 minutes in a covered bowl.
2. Toss all the berries with cherries another bowl and set it aside.
3. Stir cook wine with pomegranate juice in a saucepan.
4. Add the strained tea liquid to the saucepan.
5. Toss in the mixed berries and mix them well.
6. Enjoy.

HONEY GLAZED PEARS

If you are up for a fruity dessert after a meal, then these roasted pears with a sweet honey glaze is a perfect option. The pears are first baked in their own nectar along with butter and zest then they are served with creamy mascarpone and pistachios.

Preparation time: 10 minutes	**Cooking time:** 25 minutes	**Allergens:** Dairy

NUTRITION FACTS

Serving 3	
Amount per serving	
Calories	349
	% Daily Value*
Total Fat 14.3g	18%
Saturated Fat 8.4g	42%
Cholesterol 41mg	14%
Sodium 108mg	5%
Total Carbohydrate 53.6g	19%
Dietary Fiber 5.8g	21%
Total Sugars 41.5g	
Protein 6g	
Vitamin D 5mcg	27%
Calcium 109mg	8%
Iron 1mg	4%
Potassium 251mg	5%

INGREDIENTS

- 3 ripe medium pears, peeled, halved, and cored
- 1/4 cup pear nectar
- 3 tablespoons honey
- 2 tablespoons almond butter
- 1 teaspoon orange zest
- ½ cup mascarpone cheese
- 1/3 cup chopped roasted, salted pistachios
- Dollop of cream (optional)

INSTRUCTIONS

1. Let your oven preheat at 400° F (204° C)
2. Spread the sliced pear in a baking pan with their cut sides down.
3. Pour honey, butter, nectar and orange zest on top.
4. Roast these pears for 25 mins in the preheated oven.
5. Mix sugar with mascarpone and top the baked pears with it.
6. Garnish with honey and pistachios.
7. Enjoy.

CONVERSION TABLES

Butter or Superfine Sugar

1 cup	225 g
½ cup	115 g
1/3 cup	70 g
¼ cup	60 g
2 Tbsp	30 g

Granulated Sugar, Light or Dark Brown Sugar

1 cup	200 g
½ cup	100 g
1/3 cup	70 g
¼ cup	50 g
2 Tbsp	25 g

All-purpose or Bread Flour

1 cup	150 g
½ cup	75 g
1/3 cup	50 g
¼ cup	35 g

Cake & Pastry Flour, Icing Sugar, Rice Flour or Breadcrumbs

1 cup	130 g
½ cup	65 g
1/3 cup	45 g
¼ cup	32 g

Cocoa Powder, Corn Starch, Ground Almonds

1 cup	120 g
½ cup	60 g
1/3 cup	40 g
¼ cup	30 g

Rolled Oats, Whole Pecans, Whole Walnuts

1 cup	100 g
½ cup	50 g
⅓ cup	35 g
¼ cup	25 g

Other Ingredients

Rye Flour	1 cup	120 g
Peanut butter	1 cup	250 g
Whole hazelnuts	1 cup	135 g
Whole almonds	1 cup	160 g
Sliced almonds	1 cup	100 g
Graham crumbs	1 cup	225 g
Chocolate chips	1 cup	175 g
Coconut	1 cup	100 g
Dried currants	1 cup	160 g
Raisins	1 cup	150 g
Dried cranberries	1 cup	140 g
Fresh cranberries	1 cup	110 g
Honey	1 cup	300 g
Molasses	1 cup	260 g
Pumpkin puree	1 cup	250 g

Small Measure Items

Dry yeast	1 pkg (2 ¼ tsp)	8 g
Gelatin powder	1 Tbsp (1 pkg)	7 g
Baking powder	1 tsp	3 g
Baking soda	1 tsp	5 g
Salt (fine)	1 tsp	5 g
Cinnamon & other spices (allspice, nutmeg, clove etc.)	1 tsp	3 g
Freshly grated ginger	1 Tbsp	6 g

CONCLUSION

There is a thin between healthy and tempting food these days, it is hard to distinguish which food is actually good for your health and which one is only there to tempt you with all the aromatic ingredients. Its smart choices that can save and provide you good food in reasonably tasty styles. Mediterranean diet also prescribes such variety of meal. it has to be more vegetables, fruit, fat-free meat, grain, beans, low-fat dairy, and no processed sugars to make up a complete Mediterranean meal. With diet, an active lifestyle and routine exercises are also necessary to procure the maximum benefits out of it. Mediterranean diet can simply set up your path to get a healthier meal every time, it, however, rests on us how to alter the existing eating habits as per those set standards.

Made in the USA
Middletown, DE
15 July 2019